MW00808073

To my good friend, Jacquie —

May joy and happiness follow you each and every day.

PSYCHIC COURIER

THE LIFE AND AFTERLIFE OF CLAIRVOYANT JOSEPH DELOUISE

Mary Lou Emami

MARY LOU EMAMI

FORWARD BY EDWIN F. BECKER

∞ INFINITY
PUBLISHING

Copyright © 2016 by Mary Lou Emami

Library of Congress Control Number: 2016917758

ISBN 978-1-4958-1033-6

ISBN 978-1-4958-1034-3 eBook

http://marylouemami.com
http://psychiccourier.com

First Edition

Editor: Ellen Kleiner
Book Cover Artwork by Nicole Bertagna

Published September 2016

INFINITY PUBLISHING
1094 New DeHaven Street, Suite 100
West Conshohocken, PA 19428-2713
Toll-free (877) BUY BOOK
Local Phone (610) 941-9999
Fax (610) 941-9959
Info@buybooksontheweb.com
www.buybooksontheweb.com

For Joseph

An incredible man with an amazing gift—
one that he used to help others.

Words can never express my gratitude to have known a man such as Joseph DeLouise. While assisting him in his office, I was privileged to observe firsthand the care and concern he had for others and the many lives he touched and changed for the better. His encouragement and reassurance helped me gain confidence and a rewarding purpose in life.

I cherish the memories that Joseph left me—the fascinating details of his life, his discoveries in the world of spirit, the stories of his amazing predictions, the insights he communicated while in trance, his visions of the future, and his treasured words of wisdom—all of which I now share with others.

Acknowledgments

My heartfelt appreciation and gratitude to Helen Olberg, who came to my rescue and edited the initial draft of this book. She generously gave me her time and lovingly nudged me on. I am thankful for both her help and her friendship.

Untold thanks to my dearest friend Carolyn Santucci, who tirelessly read and reread multiple passages from the work. Her input, wisdom, and encouragement were priceless—most precious, her lasting friendship.

Deepest thanks go to my good friend Sue Coulson, whose suggestion we visit a psychic set my journey in motion.

I am forever grateful to Hans Christian King, internationally acclaimed medium and spiritual teacher whose fame for communicating with the dead has earned him international recognition and gratitude. Twice while writing this work Hans channeled Joseph, giving me clarity and faith in my endeavors.

My warmest gratitude goes to Debbie Jacob, a loving and caring psychic/medium who also channeled Joseph and encouraged me to persevere in my efforts to publish.

Thanks also to Lora Lisbon, content editor who worked tirelessly to give this book structure and form, while preserving Joseph's truths and keeping his messages uppermost in mind.

My sincerest appreciation goes to Ellen Kleiner, whose phenomenal editing skills transformed my tendency to wordiness into a concise reader-friendly manuscript and who never lost sight of forwarding Joseph's mission.

Much love and thanks go to my grandson and newly published author Brad Cook, who designed my website then guided me through parts of the internet that were unfamiliar to me.

Finally, with special gratitude to those who lovingly cared for Joseph and tenderly watched over him during his last days on earth: Joseph DeLouise Jr., devotedly loving son; Linda Smith, eternally loving daughter; Amy Lauer, forever faithful "daughter"; Richard Kemp, steadfast and loyal friend; and Pat Belavarie, secretary, friend, and caretaker.

FOREWORD

Mary Lou Emami has written an amazing book. It is one long overdue. I felt it an honor to be asked to write this foreword for a book about Joseph DeLouise. He was an amazing man. God sometimes awards individuals with special gifts—gifts that God knows will be used to benefit others and He chose well with Joseph.

Unlike the author, my wife Marsha and I were not involved closely throughout Joseph's life, but for a number of years that we clung to him. At a time when he was prominent in the media and was a nationally known psychic celebrity, he recognized that a young couple with no means were in trouble. He stepped away from many important commitments and came to our aid. He diagnosed malevolent spirits that included one he admitted was beyond his capability to deal with. He called for an exorcist to assist in cleansing our building. The hours he spent were many, and more time was spent counseling us to change our behavior in facing these things with compassion, respect, and faith in God. Though it was filmed by NBC, Joseph never called for media attention and refused a post-exorcism interview to promote his book, *Psychic Mission*.

He remained a close friend for many years. I came to understand the burden of what some call a 'gift.' I saw firsthand the frustrations of knowing something disastrous was going to happen, yet not knowing exactly where, or when. Joseph carried this burden throughout his life. He exhibited a genuine kindness that is so very rare. As I once told him, "If I had your gifts, I would not tell a soul." This, because he faced continuous ridicule and doubt by people with no understanding of these tremendous abilities. When I joined him on the Jack Eigen radio show as a naive young man, I had no idea Joseph was to become comedy relief. Afterward, I asked, "How do you tolerate that?" He just smiled and stated, "I am used to facing people who don't believe or understand." That was Joseph. He faced skepticism, ridicule, and doubt with kindness. A true psychic cannot turn it on and off like the radio since the visions come without warning. The psychic carries the anxiety of sometimes not receiving all the facts and having to fill in the blanks. At times the feeling of desperation in wanting to warn people can be almost unbearable.

Though we were close for a number of years, I never asked him about my future. I enjoyed him as a friend and as a very intelligent man who loved a good laugh and I hope I provided him with a few. In speaking with him in his later years, I could sense the burden was wearing him down, but he never gave in and always moved forward. I hope now that his work is over he knows that he was loved and respected by many, many people whom he helped and that their lives are a bit brighter because he was there for them. My book *True Haunting* was dedicated to him. Mary Lou's book tells his story and offers insight to the psychic world. It is an important work and one to which I am honored to contribute.

Edwin F. Becker, 2015

List of Illustrations

PREFACE

Renowned Chicago psychic Joseph DeLouise was a trance clairvoyant and medium, meaning that he received his visions while in trance—something I had the honor to witness on numerous occasions.

Nearly all of Joseph's visions were of tragedies. It was difficult for him to observe these horrific events and feel the fear of the victims, knowing he was unable to prevent the disasters from occurring; knowing they were destined to manifest.

His predictions centered on current events, not incidents that would take place in some future century. The accuracy of his visions earned Joseph titles such as *"Dean of Psychics," "Prophet of Specifics," "Mr. I Told You So."*

Joseph demonstrated his amazing foresight in predictions such as the Ted Kennedy-Mary Jo Kopechne drowning, the collapse of the Silver Bridge (of *Mothman* fame), Wall Street's Black Monday, and, remarkably, the fall of the Berlin Wall.

Later predictions included the resurgence of maritime piracy, a royal funeral procession, a black market for body organs, the 9/11 terrorist attack, the United States movement toward a police state, *"possibly a sort of dictatorship,"* people struggling with unemployment, taxes, rising food costs and more—leading to revolts, *"maybe even a revolution,"* and a scandal around Hillary Clinton and mail.

Equally impressive were details he provided to police regarding the Sharon Tate murders, as well as his insights into the Zodiac Killer.

Joseph did not restrict himself to headline-making predictions. He used the power of his mind to develop his ability to travel out-of-body to otherworldly realms. These astral travels afforded him the opportunity to explore the afterlife and uncover secrets in the world of spirit.

In one such astral travel he observed the passage of time in a dimension where the past, the present and the future exist together. As Joseph explained, "All things take place first in Spirit before they manifest here in our physical world. This strange characteristic of time makes it possible to foresee future events, yet difficult to pinpoint precisely when they will take place on earth."

Joseph was a spiritual man whose upbringing instilled in him a desire to help others. A compassionate spiritual teacher and psychic, he was much beloved by his many loyal clients. It was Joseph's desire to take away the fear of death and bring others proof of an afterlife.

He helped me overcome my shyness, find my first job, grow as a professional, and excel at my work. I eventually became his assistant, which allowed me to witness firsthand the positive impact he had on others.

In *Psychic Courier,* you will find the stories of Joseph's life as he told them to me throughout the many years of our friendship and professional association— his experiences of ESP, the truths and principles he grew up with, the numerous out-of-body discoveries he made while exploring spiritual realms, and the fascinating stories behind his amazing visions. The following pages feature many messages he would want to share with others.

I hope that readers enjoy and find inspiration in his incredible story.

PART I

EARLY PREDICTIONS

THE SILVER BRIDGE DISASTER

Joseph DeLouise, owner of a beauty shop in Chicago, made public the first of his major predictions on November 25, 1967, on the Warren Freiberg radio program *The Strangest People in the World*, broadcast over WWCA out of Gary, Indiana. This was Joseph's second appearance as a guest on Freiberg's show.

The first time had been a few weeks earlier, soon after Freiberg's aunt had visited Joseph's beauty salon and asked Joseph a few questions about her future. Whatever he said impressed her, and she excitedly told the radio host about the psychic hairdresser in Chicago whose insights were right on target. Freiberg subsequently invited Joseph to be a guest on the program's October 1967 Halloween special. This was forty-year-old Joseph's first time on radio, and he didn't know what to expect. It did not go well.

Joseph talked about his psychic experiences, and of course, Freiberg requested that Joseph make a prediction. During the station break Joseph focused on the crystal ball he'd brought with him, attempting to see a vision of the future. When no vision appeared, Joseph told Freiberg that he wasn't getting anything and went on to explain that such visions were spontaneous—they didn't come at a psychic's command.

This explanation did not seem to satisfy Freiberg, who'd been hoping for something more exciting for his listeners. Freiberg was a skeptic, and Joseph's response simply confirmed his opinion. He told his audience that he could not remember any of the so-called psychics he'd had on his program saying or doing anything that would prove to him they were genuine, and he doubted that any ever would. Joseph's first appearance on the radio ended poorly.

Despite that, he was invited back for the November 25th show. Freiberg told his audience that with Thanksgiving approaching he was feeling generous and had offered Mr. DeLouise a second chance, but warned him he'd better do something to prove he wasn't a phony or it would be his last invitation to be on the show.

This time Joseph was prepared. As soon as he had received Freiberg's second invitation, he picked up his crystal ball and placed it on the table in front of him. He stared into it—nothing. He tried again—still nothing came through. He was having trouble relaxing his mind.

Joseph didn't need a crystal ball to foresee a future event. He only used it to focus his attention and calm his mind. Normally, all he had to do was relax and something would come through. However, after his first failure with Freiberg, he felt tense. Gradually he managed to clear his mind, and on the third try a vision appeared.

Far from insignificant, this vision was startling and gruesome. It so shocked Joseph that he covered the crystal ball and left the room. Meditating the next day, he saw the same disturbing vision, which told Joseph it was inevitable—this event would soon materialize in the physical world.

The week passed slowly. Saturday, November 25 seemed as if it would never arrive. But the day did arrive, and Joseph was nervous, thinking this was his last chance. Joseph listened as Freiberg reminded his audience of Mr. DeLouise's appearance on the Halloween show the month before and how nothing in particular had come of it—nothing that would prove he was psychic. Freiberg did most of the talking, and it wasn't flattering. Just prior to the break, Freiberg reiterated his warning and asked Joseph if he would have a prediction for his audience; Joseph replied that he would.

Off-air, Joseph took out his crystal ball and placed it on the table in front of him. He stilled his mind and stared into the crystal. As the program resumed, Joseph was already in a trance, once again seeing exactly the same vision he had seen days before. The first scene showed water stirred by the wind. As he continued to watch, a bridge slowly came into view, waves slapping against its concrete pilings. Heavy traffic was crossing the bridge. Joseph sensed it was late in the day, probably rush hour.

The scene soon shifted, zooming in on concrete pilings that supported the bridge. Joseph had the impression that the pilings were rotting. As he watched, a crack appeared. It spread and then grew larger until the pilings began to crumble. Lurching, the bridge buckled and gave way. A large section collapsed into the water, along with dozens of people trapped inside their vehicles. Some, managing to get free of their cars, were hanging onto the bridge.

The scene shifted again, and now Joseph witnessed cars rolling off the bridge and into the water. As they plunged over the edge, he caught a glimpse of the license plates. The corner of each plate was imprinted, in small digits, with the number *1967*. Joseph was convinced that the disaster would take place that year.

While in trance, Joseph could hear words and sounds as easily as he saw images. He now heard the screams of people as they tumbled toward the frigid, rushing water. Sounds amplified and images of the victims magnified as if making certain to draw his attention to the emotional impact of this tragedy. The screams of the victims were even more disturbing to Joseph than the dreadful scenes he viewed.

He saw the people on land jump from their cars, rushing to help those who had toppled from the bridge. Watching in horror, they could do nothing. The churning water swiftly dispatched its screaming victims, swallowing passengers trapped inside their cars as well as those who had escaped from their vehicles.

Coming out of trance, Joseph heard Freiberg repeating to his audience all that he had said. Without realizing it, Joseph had been speaking aloud throughout the entire trance, giving details of his vision. Freiberg seemed visibly impressed and a little upset. His attitude toward Joseph had definitely changed.

Now speaking in a reverent tone, Freiberg explained to the audience what had just taken place. Reiterating for his listeners the things Joseph had said during trance, he stated that this was the first and only time a psychic had done anything to make him take notice.

Freiberg wanted to know where the bridge was and when this event would take place. Joseph told him it wasn't a famous bridge, but it was large and somewhere southeast of Chicago. The piles on the bridge were rotting, he said, and he believed the bridge would collapse before the end of the year.

It seemed that Freiberg could hardly believe what he had heard. The end of the year was just five weeks away. This was a very bold prediction. He told his audience that he had his doubts. They must all wait and see.

Weeks passed with no word of the collapse. Joseph kept going back and forth, tormented by thoughts of the tragedy and tortured by fear of failure. He questioned the reality of the vision and his feeling of certainty that it would happen. He suffered the burden of his gift. Who would want to predict such a thing while being powerless to prevent it? He wondered why he had been given this gift. How was he supposed to use it?

As he waited for 1967 to draw to a close, he fervently hoped that his prediction would not come to pass even if Freiberg made him look like a fraud.

On December 15, 1967—three weeks after Joseph's vision—Silver Bridge, spanning the Ohio River between West Virginia and Ohio, collapsed at Point Pleasant, West Virginia, killing forty-six persons.

On that day Joseph had left his shop early. A feeling of foreboding had come over him as his intuition told him his vision had materialized. At home, the phone rang. On hearing the news, Joseph could hardly speak—the tragedy had taken place exactly as he had seen it. Joseph was both elated at this and filled with guilt over his inability to stop the event from occurring. Joseph fervently wished he had never made the prediction public. Then Freiberg called to congratulate him, but added that if Joseph could provide him with yet another prediction, he could be more certain of his psychic powers.

Following the Silver Bridge tragedy, Joseph traveled to Point Pleasant. He'd heard that locals were convinced that a strange creature, a creature known as "Mothman"[1] had been its cause. Naturally, he wanted to investigate.

On arriving, he found Point Pleasant to be a tight-knit community. Word spread quickly that a mysterious stranger dressed in black (Joseph was wearing a black hat and black overcoat) was asking questions. At first Joseph had a difficult time getting anyone to talk; however, when residents discovered he was the man who had predicted the collapse of the bridge, doors began to open. Residents were eager to meet the man with mystical powers.

Joseph told me that those who had seen the creature said it was more than seven feet tall and looked like a man, but had the face of a moth, was feathered, and had wings. Some described the wings as gigantic, while others alluded to a wingspan of eight to ten feet. The creature's eyes were red and glowed in the dark, they said. Some claimed it swooped down on them.

Others who had encountered the creature while driving their cars talked of the creature's tremendous speed. They said that no matter how fast they drove to get away, the Mothman kept up, menacingly dive-bombing them. As terrifying as the creature was, it did no apparent harm to anyone with whom Joseph spoke. Joseph had seen no such creature in his vision, but he kept an open mind.

The following March, an article describing Joseph's prediction of the Silver Bridge collapse appeared in *New Age World* newspaper (see Figure 1).

ESP 'vision' of bridge disaster told

CHICAGO DAILY NEWS,

Cranes continue to haul cars from the Ohio River following Friday's disastrous bridge collapse. (AP)

The combination of a Gary radio program and the recent West Virginia bridge disaster has overnight made a celebrity of hairdresser Joseph DeLouise. It was on the Warren Freiburg Show over radio station WWCA on November 25th 1967 that DeLouise predicted: "Before the end of the year, a major bridge - not as large as the Brooklyn or Golden Gate bridges, but a large one - will collapse, causing a great number of deaths and making newspaper headlines." When the "Silver Bridge" spanning the Ohio River at Point Pleasant, West Virginia, collapsed, DeLouise found himself pursued by representatives of the press, radio, and television.

The 40-year-old hairdresser is still a bit taken aback by his sudden fame. DeLouise has known for some years of his facility for ESP (or extra-sensory perception). Friends recall that Joseph also predicted Kennedy's assassination and the McCormick Place fire. Many of these same friends had consulted him on personal problems. Like fellow-psychic Jeane Dixon, DeLouise uses a crystal ball for much of his psychic work, but also receives impressions without its aid. "The main thing," he says, "is deep meditation. It takes me quite a period of

PSYCHIC PREDICTION OF THE YEAR

Story by DAVID TECHTER

concentrating before I get clear impressions. I don't like to take the time unless the matter is important enough."

He is quite an evangelist for psychic matters and has appeared on radio shows in New York City and Des Moines, Iowa, as well as Gary and Chicago. Amongst his predictions for 1968 is that beards will become more fashionable, and DeLouise has already started the trend.

Figure 1. New Age World article featuring Joseph's prediction of the Silver Bridge disaster.

VISION OF A TRAIN CRASH

D ecember 14, 1968, was a chilly but pleasant day. Joseph hummed a tune as he drove to pick up his friend Reverend Fred Haase, a member of the Independent Spiritualist Church where both men were ordained ministers. Members of spiritualist churches practice Spiritualism, a belief system that encourages living in harmony with God's laws—natural laws believed to be just, impartial, consistent, and nonjudgmental. Governing the visible and the invisible, the living and the dead, these laws maintain order in the universe.

Joseph and Reverend Fred shared a mutual interest in ESP, which formed an immediate bond between them. Fred was also a medium, meaning that he could communicate with those who had died. Together he and Joseph performed exorcisms, releasing earthbound entities to the spirit world. Joseph and Fred would eventually become frequent guests on many radio and television programs.

On this day they were travelling to Gary, Indiana, to be guests on Warren Freiberg's radio broadcast of *The Strangest People in the World,* making this Joseph's third appearance and Fred's first. Stepping into the car, Fred mentioned that it was a good day for traveling so the trip shouldn't take long—a prediction that was soon proved wrong!

During the trip, Joseph told Fred about an article he was to submit the next day to the *Chicago Sun-Times* as part of a feature on predictions for 1969. He explained that following the collapse of the Silver Bridge, the media had taken notice of him. The newspaper had invited him to contribute this article and would be coming to interview and photograph him. Excited about the prospect of appearing in a newspaper special, Joseph had begun meditating on future events.

In the article, he planned to mention one vision that had come to him a month earlier, about two trains colliding head-on in the fog. He believed they were on the Illinois Central line. Joseph asked Fred to write down this prediction, as well as others that had come to his mind.

As they drew closer to Gary, Joseph glanced at the car's temperature gauge and noticed that, in spite of the brisk weather, the needle was starting to rise. He pulled to the side of the road and shut the engine off to let the radiator cool. Immediately, Joseph's thoughts turned to the article slated for submission the following day. As his gaze focused on the windshield, it clouded; suddenly, a vision flashed into his mind. Resting his head on the steering wheel, Joseph called softly to Fred, who, realizing that Joseph was going into a trance, grabbed a pencil and prepared to record Joseph's words. He wrote:

> "I'm riding on a train. It's bouncing and swerving. People are screaming. Now the car I'm riding in is jackknifing, tipping over. Terrible heat is coming from somewhere—the train must be on fire! I hear more screams, cries of pain.
>
> Many people are lying on the ground. Others are trying to help those who are injured. It's dark and foggy. I feel dizzy, disoriented; as if I'm about to black out."

After a few minutes, Joseph came out of his trance and told Fred he had seen the same vision a few weeks earlier—only today's vision was more detailed; not only was he watching as the two trains collided, he was "living" the event as it happened. This time he was riding in one of the cars and became dizzy when the train started to jolt; disoriented as the car rolled onto its side. He heard moaning and saw people picking through the rubble to help the injured. Just as he felt he might black out, Joseph saw the words "Illinois Central" on the side of one of the cars.

Fred and Joseph continued to talk until Joseph felt fully alert. Then, worried about being late for the show, he raced through the streets of Gary to the radio station, wondering how Freiberg would view this new prediction. Would it be with his usual skepticism?

To Joseph's surprise, on the radio broadcast Freiberg introduced him without cynicism and retold the story of the Silver Bridge collapse. Freiberg then asked Joseph to share his latest predictions.

Joseph then related his predictions of winning sports teams, what he saw for Hollywood celebrities, the severity of the current winter season, and at the very end, his vision of a train accident in the Midwest that would happen very soon. Freiberg immediately broke in and asked Joseph to elaborate, at which point he related the details of his vision just as he had related them to Fred. After explaining that the crash would happen on a very foggy night and that two trains would be involved, he added that the accident would occur early the next year somewhere south of Chicago; he concluded by saying that many people would be hurt and, sadly, some would die. When Joseph finished speaking, Freiberg told his audience that if this vision came to pass, Joseph would make a believer out of him.

When Joseph submitted his predictions to the *Chicago Sun-Times* on the following day, December 15, 1968, he included his vision of the train crash, naming the Illinois Central Railroad. Subsequently an editor called to request permission to omit the name of the railroad. Joseph agreed. The article that appeared on December 29, 1968, in *Midwest Magazine*, a Sunday supplement of the *Chicago Sun-Times*, was altered to read: "a terrible train wreck south of Chicago."[2]

Within weeks, Joseph would receive a disturbing phone call regarding this prediction.

VISION OF A DROWNING

An even more astonishing vision came to Joseph at the interview itself. On the following day, December 15, 1968, Joseph, astrologer Annette Wilson [with whom Joseph shared an office], the *Chicago Sun-Times* editor, and the newspaper photographer, talked after shooting pictures at Joseph's beauty shop. Weary from the day's activities, Joseph sat down to rest, whereupon the photographer asked for a picture of Joseph gazing into a crystal ball. Stretching and yawning, Joseph, with his eyes half closed, glanced into the crystal ball on the table next to him. Suddenly the crystal filled with mist, and just as quickly a vision appeared.

Mrs. Wilson, who was familiar with Joseph's visionary gifts, could see he was going into trance and quickly hushed the others. As they gathered round, Joseph began talking. His voice was soft. The two newspapermen leaned close and listened in wonder, hardly able to believe what they were hearing as Joseph described what he was seeing.

He spoke softly, saying that he saw a woman; a woman drowning. He said there were bubbles coming out of her mouth, her nose, her eyes—and her hair was softly streaming away from her face as she slowly sank down in the water.

When Joseph emerged from his trance, the two men, shocked and amazed, were staring at him incredulously. Joseph explained that the drowning woman was somehow associated with Senator Ted Kennedy and that, while he saw her face clearly, he did not recognize her. Then he added, "I saw a newspaper headline. It read: 'Ted Kennedy,' then blank space, blank space, then the word 'Drowns.'"

When the *Chicago Sun-Times* December 29, 1968, article, "What Psychics See for 1969" was published, the prediction read, "A tragedy around water involving the Kennedys."[2]

A Disturbing Phone Call
and a Visit from the Dead

———

I n January, when radio shows typically feature topics that center on the New Year's theme, Joseph repeated the Kennedy prediction on several programs. He again spoke of the potential for a terrible accident on the Illinois Central Railroad. A few days after one such program, Joseph received a phone call from a man who'd heard him speak. The man didn't give his name but he told Joseph that he was an engineer with the Illinois Central Railroad. He wanted to talk about the train crash that Joseph had been predicting.

The man began by telling Joseph he knew his prediction about a bad train accident was correct. He said that for a long time he'd had the feeling that two trains would collide and that one of them would be his. He went on to say he knew the accident was bound to happen and nothing could change the outcome.

Joseph tried to calm the man by telling him that a premonition doesn't necessarily mean the event is destined to happen. He went on to say that from time to time he himself experienced foreboding over an event that never came about, adding that his visions were not always correct. However, no matter how he tried, nothing Joseph said comforted the man. Although he didn't let on, Joseph knew with certainty the inevitable—that this man would be involved in the train crash revealed in his vision.

Continuing, the man told Joseph that he believed this was his fate and no one could do anything to change it. Joseph also believed that some events are beyond our control and it is just a matter of time until they occur. The man went on, "I haven't said anything to my wife about what I feel. It'll be hard enough for her to hear about it when it happens." The man ended the call by thanking Joseph for talking with him, adding it was a relief to be able to speak with someone about the situation.

As days went by, the man's voice haunted Joseph; he found it difficult to shake off his feelings of foreboding. On the night of January 16, 1969, as Joseph was preparing to leave the beauty shop, a familiar sense of apprehension swept over him. He left hurriedly, anxious to get home. However, on stepping outside, Joseph saw that a dense fog had moved in and covered everything. There was no way he'd be able to get home quickly. The fog was so thick he could barely see well enough to drive.

An eerie feeling came over Joseph. He was certain that tonight was the night the train crash would occur. The fog and his thoughts of the crash took everything out of him. Upon arriving home, he turned on the news—not a word about a train wreck. He switched channels. Still nothing.

He wanted to be wrong, and yet Joseph was certain it had happened. Throwing on his coat, he ran to a nearby store and asked to see the evening papers. There was no news of a train wreck in any of them. Joseph grumbled, "Nothing on television, nothing in the newspapers."

Aware that Joseph received premonitions, shopkeeper Joseph Stimac asked him if he needed help. Joseph hollered, "Where's the paper with news of the train wreck?"

"Train wreck?" Stimac asked. "I've seen nothing about a train wreck." With a look of concern, he asked Joseph if he'd had another vision.

Annoyed that his search was fruitless, Joseph left without replying. Back home, he crawled onto the couch and fell into a deep sleep. About two a.m., a man with tears in his eyes woke him up. He looked strange—nearly transparent and oddly luminous. It was foggy but Joseph could see something was going on behind the man. As he stood there, the man told Joseph that tonight was the night. He sobbed and said, "It's too bad for my family. But there isn't anything I can do about it now." Soon after that, he faded away.

Joseph lurched awake. He sat straight up, realizing this had been more than a just a dream—it was vivid, surreal. He was sure the man he had just seen was the same man who telephoned about the wreck. His appearance was strangely unreal—he was dead, yet still he had communicated.

Sitting alone in the dark, Joseph felt remorse at knowing another disaster he'd foreseen had struck again.

On January 17, 1969, the morning headline in the *Chicago Daily News* read, "Trains Collide, 3 Killed." The article explained that an Illinois Central passenger train, *The Campus*, a commuter train that served students studying at Southern Illinois University, had crashed head-on with a freight train, killing three and injuring forty-nine. The crash occurred at Manteno, about forty-five miles south of Chicago. Officials believed that, due to the dense fog, one of the engineers missed a switch signal. The paper gave the name of two engineers—William Coffey, operating the passenger train, and Richard W. Dinkleman, operating the freight train.

As Joseph later explained in an interview with Harold Hill of the *National Insider*, "I did not investigate which engineer had contacted me; I had the experience and was convinced of its authenticity—this was good enough for me."[3] If Joseph knew which engineer had contacted him, he obviously decided to keep it private.

When interviewed about the train crash, shopkeeper Joseph Stimac confirmed that Joseph had come to his store on the night of the accident looking for a newspaper that told of the train crash. In a signed statement he said: "It was about 10:30 p.m. when he [Joseph] came in asking for the latest newspaper, stating that he wanted the one with the train wreck headlines. I told him I had not heard of any train wreck. That night I told my wife about it and the next morning, to our surprise, all three papers carried headlines of the train wreck south of Chicago."[4]

Also interviewed was psychic buff David Techter, who had been a guest on Freiberg's radio program when Joseph made the train crash prediction. Techter stated: "Among other predictions, DeLouise said that there would be a serious train wreck early in the year in the Midwest. When pressed for further details, he volunteered that it would involve two trains, that it would take place on a foggy night, that many lives would be lost and that it would make headlines in the Chicago newspapers."[5]

CHAPPAQUIDDICK

Saturday, July 19, 1969, began like any other day. By now the intensity of Joseph's visions had prepared him to expect the unexpected, and today would not disappoint.

The phone rang. Tony DeLise, Joseph's friend from childhood, was on the line. Tony was breathless, as if he had taken a punch to the stomach. He finally blurted out, "Joe, it's happened just like you said it would!" Tony took a deep breath and went on, "Last night. The drowning—it's all over the news. Turn on your radio, Joe!"

According to radio reports, Senator Ted Kennedy was involved in an accident with Mary Jo Kopechne in which the car he was driving plunged off a bridge. He made several rescue attempts but was unable to save her. Kennedy escaped, but Mary Jo drowned.

Later reports revealed that on July 18, 1969, Kennedy was on the island of Chappaquiddick for the annual sailing regatta. After the race, he headed to a rented cottage where he cohosted a cookout for a small group of people who had worked on the Robert F. Kennedy campaign. Among those invited were six young women, dubbed as the "boiler-room girls," since their desks were housed in the mechanical room of the campaign headquarters. One of these young women was Mary Jo Kopechne.

The news media were all over the story with details that went something like this:

Kennedy left the party early. When he announced he was leaving, Mary Jo asked if he would drop her off at her hotel. Strangely, she told no one where she was going and left her pocketbook at the cottage. Kennedy said he was headed for the ferry and made a wrong turn onto Dike Road, an unlit, unpaved dirt road that led to Dike Bridge, a wooden slat bridge with no guardrails. Realizing that he had reached the bridge, Kennedy said he applied the brakes but it was too late and the car dove over the side of the bridge, plunged into the water, and landed upside-down on its roof.

Kennedy freed himself from the car, but Mary Jo could not. On reaching the surface, he called out her name. When there was no answer, he dove down repeatedly trying several times to free her but was unable. After resting a few minutes, he walked back to the cottage and got his cousin, Joe Gargan, and party cohost, Paul Markham, to return with him to try to rescue Kopechne. Their efforts failed. Kennedy ordered the two men back to the party, telling them not to say anything; that he would take care of the accident. Kennedy swam across the channel in a state of shock and returned to his hotel on Edgartown.

At 8:15 the next morning, two fishermen spotted the submerged car and the authorities were notified. Police Chief James Arena arrived within minutes and summoned John Farrar, a professional diver who arrived fully dressed in diving suit. He promptly extricated Mary Jo's body from the car. Farrar felt that if a proper rescue attempt had been made in a timely manner, she would have survived.

At 10:00 a.m. in the morning, Kennedy went to the police station in Edgartown to report the incident. At the station, Kennedy told the police about the accident and how after several unsuccessful attempts to save Mary Jo, he walked back to the cottage and crawled into the backseat of a car in a state of exhaustion and shock. He then asked for someone to bring him back to Edgartown where he walked around for a period of time and then went back to his hotel room. In the morning, when he fully realized what had happened, he said he immediately contacted the police.

On July 25, seven days after the incident, Kennedy pleaded guilty of leaving the scene of an accident and causing injury. Kennedy's attorneys suggested that any jail sentence should be suspended. Prosecutors agreed to this, citing Kennedy's age, character, and prior reputation. Judge James Boyle sentenced Kennedy to two months' incarceration, the statutory minimum for the offense, which he suspended.

On July 21, two days after Joseph received the call from his friend about the Chappaquiddick incident, Joseph received a second phone call related to the tragedy. This one was from the editor of the *National Enquirer*, who, recalling the article published there months earlier, remarked that Joseph was the only psychic in the world to have made the prediction about Kennedy being involved in a drowning. The editor asked Joseph to fly to Massachusetts to pick up additional impressions of the incident.

When he first heard news of the drowning, Joseph had become depressed at again having foreseen a tragedy without being able to intervene. Excitement was now layered upon despair. It felt flattering to be recognized by a national publication. This story was important. People the world over were concerned with the details. Many had questions about the accident that remained unanswered. The question uppermost in nearly everyone's mind was why Kennedy had waited until the next day to report the incident to the police.

On July 29, the *National Enquirer* flew Joseph to Martha's Vineyard, where he was met by Harry Edgington, one of its reporters. The men checked into a hotel, rented a car, and took the Edgartown-Chappaquiddick ferry across the 200-yard channel. Disembarking, they drove the short distance to the cottage where the party immediately preceding the tragic accident had been held. While driving along the winding road, Joseph grew fidgety. Even though ten days had passed since the accident, Joseph could feel the strong emotions surrounding the event. Arriving at the cottage where the party had taken place, Joseph and Edgington found the front door open and went inside.

As Joseph surveyed the interior of the cottage, the reporter watched him carefully, ready to take notes on his every word, his body language, and his reactions. Joseph told Edgington that he sensed several people had been there having a good time. However, as he approached one of the bedrooms, sensations associated with lies and deception began to crowd into his mind. Joseph heard quarreling. When he opened the bedroom door, the intensity of the quarreling increased. Joseph felt as if he had been caught in the middle of a battlefield. Crying and shouting exploded in his mind as the voices escalated into rage and then quickly turned to shock and disbelief. No longer able to endure the wrath, Joseph turned to leave. As he stepped outside, he heard a woman weeping.

Joseph and Edgington then drove to the bridge where the accident had taken place. Once again Joseph was besieged by emotions—the terror that Mary Jo felt as she struggled to get out of the car, her panic, and her thoughts of wanting to "get out—get out of there." Joseph felt Mary Jo's desperation as she clung to life, hope waning with each minute that passed. Hurrying back to the car, Joseph told Edgington that he couldn't remain there any longer, that he had to leave.

Years later, when Joseph shared with me his perception of the events that took place on that fateful night, he said his psychic clairvoyance had shown him that Mary Jo was quarreling with a man at the party. Kennedy stepped in and tried to defuse the argument by suggesting the three of them drive to find a private place to talk. As Mary Jo drove, the argument escalated and tempers flared. Joseph felt that despite Kennedy's attempt to calm things, Mary Jo was becoming more and more distressed—so much so that she finally stopped the car and asked the two men to get out, telling them she wanted to be alone. They agreed and began walking back to the cottage.

Joseph saw that in her distraught condition, Mary Jo drove away with her foot pressed down hard on the gas pedal. The car accelerated, leaped onto the narrow plank bridge, and sped forward. Kennedy watched in horror as the car swerved, plunged into the water, and quickly sank to the bottom. Joseph saw that Kennedy ran to the spot where the car went over and dove several times trying to rescue her. Joseph said he could feel the terror experienced by both Mary Jo and Kennedy at his repeated, failed attempts to get her out of the car.

Although Kennedy testified under oath that he was driving the car on the night of the accident, Joseph disagreed. He told me, "As soon as I stepped out of the car onto the bridge, my psychic 'radar' kicked in. I knew beyond a doubt that Mary Jo was driving the car when it plunged into the water."

In a later interview with columnist Arnold Weissmann, Joseph again mentioned that it was Mary Jo driving the vehicle. Weissmann included this interview in "Tales of the Psychic City," an article printed in *Reader* on April 30, 1976, where Joseph was quoted as saying:

> "Ted Kennedy was not in the car when Mary Jo Kopechne drove off the bridge. She got angry at Ted before they got to the bridge, kicked him out of the car, and then accidentally drove off the bridge. Ted did try to save her. The government is holding information about the case over Kennedy's head so that he won't run for president."[6]

Joseph's claim that the reporting of the incident would interfere with Kennedy's ability to run for president was confirmed in an article by freelance writer Jennifer L. Goss in about.com's *about education* section:

Ted Kennedy and the Chappaquiddick Accident

A Car Accident That Killed a Young Woman and Kennedy's Political Ambitions

"Aside from the tarnish on his reputation, the only immediate impact of this incident on Ted Kennedy was a temporary suspension of his driver's license, ending in November 1970. This inconvenience would pale in comparison to the effects on his reputation....

"In 1979, Kennedy began the motions towards challenging incumbent Jimmy Carter for the Democratic Party nomination. Carter selectively referenced the incident at Chappaquiddick and Kennedy ended up losing to him during the primary campaign."[7]

Many internet articles have been written on this tragic event. Books exposing the Chappaquiddick tragedy include *The Kennedy Men: Three Generations of Sex, Scandal, and Secrets* by Nellie Bly; *Senatorial Privilege: The Chappaquiddick Cover-up* by Leo Damore; and *The Bridge at Chappaquiddick* by Jack Olsen.

While talking with me about this incident, Joseph stopped often, as if hesitant to go on. I could see he was still visibly shaken by Mary Jo's panic at not being able to escape from the car and by the terror she felt while awaiting the rescue that never came. At such times, I realized that Joseph not only saw imagery in his visions but physically took on the pain and terror experienced by the victims of each tragedy.

Flashback: Vision of a Plane Crash

On a cold winter's day late in January 1969, as Joseph gazed into his crystal, the image of a blue sky appeared. A large cottonlike cloud floated into view. Joseph relaxed. Unlike his usual visions, this one seemed quiet and blissful.

Then, just when he thought he'd see no tragedy, Joseph heard a buzzing sound from what seemed to be the engine of a private plane that was nowhere in sight. Suddenly, a large passenger plane came into view. It flew straight into the side of the soft cloud and disappeared in the mist. Within moments a blast shook Joseph—the *whumph* from the explosion sucking out his breath.

Dozens of metal shards burst from the cloud, followed by a huge portion of the plane that plunged straight to the earth below. In his mind the numbers *330* and *79* appeared. Joseph felt the plane would crash somewhere in the Midwest. His final impression—*Indianapolis* or *Indiana*.

Joseph first announced this prediction on February 25, 1969, while appearing as a guest of radio host Eddie Hubbard, whose program was broadcast over WGN Chicago to an audience of over 800,000. Joseph repeated his prediction on May 20, 1969, on Bob Allard's radio program broadcast on WOC in Davenport, Iowa. On both shows he told listeners he wasn't certain about the number *330*, adding that he didn't know if it was the time of day the accident would happen or the flight number of the plane. On the Hubbard show Joseph said he felt certain that seventy-nine passengers would be killed.

❈

On September 9, 1969, the headline of the evening edition of the Chicago *Sun-Times* newspaper read, *"Midair crash! Jet with Eighty-Two Falls near*

Indianapolis." The vision that Joseph had foreseen eight months before was the September 9, 1969 head-on collision of an Allegheny Airlines jet and a single-engine Piper Cherokee over Shelbyville, Indiana. The story indicated that an Allegheny airlines DC-9 carrying seventy-eight passengers and a crew of four collided with a small private plane that was piloted by a student. No one survived. Shaken to see his prediction in print, he faced the terrible reality that yet another tragic vision had materialized.

Joseph hurried home with the newspaper. As he drove, he wondered about the number seventy-eight. He had told Eddie Hubbard that he saw seventy-nine passengers would be killed. However, he quickly dismissed the thought, knowing that visions were not always easy to interpret. Just as the meaning of the number *330* was not clear, at times Joseph would see a headline that was incomplete, as in the Kennedy-Kopechne vision, where he could see a newspaper headline but some of the words were missing or blanked out. Although he sensed a string of words, he could see only the words *Ted Kennedy* and *Drowns*. It was when he saw the face of a drowning woman that Joseph was able to put the pieces together and make the prediction more accurate.

Joseph had told me, "Things that come through in a vision are not always clear. There are times when the scenes in a vision don't show the whole picture. Visions don't always come through in the way you would expect. A fleeting image might appear and, a moment later, disappear; images with no apparent relationship might show up; the presentation of details may not be in an orderly sequence. It's left to the psychic to interpret what he or she has been shown."

At home, Joseph pushed the thought of the air disaster out of his mind—that is, he thought he did. He went to bed early. As he slept, a dream came to him—one he would never forget. In the dream a plane landed gently on a cloud. A stairway rolled up to the door and passengers began to disembark. As they reached the last step, each looked up at Joseph as if silently bidding him goodbye. Joseph counted them as they passed. "Seventy-eight." *I was wrong this time*, he thought. Just then a woman who had passed him before returned and stood next to Joseph. As she did, she turned sideways and pointed to the bulge beneath her dress, which clearly showed she was with child. Here was number seventy-nine!

After going public with his predictions, Joseph began to attract national attention. Some people said he was a jinx and blamed him for the accidents. Of course, Joseph questioned why, as a person with an upbeat nature, was he seeing these horrific visions. He hated that people thought of him as a bearer of bad news and felt great frustration at being able to foresee tragedies that he was unable to prevent. The plane crash was now the third such tragedy in a row. Being a prophet of doom so greatly disturbed Joseph that he nearly gave up on his psychic work.

However, thinking more on it, the thought came to him that he might have been given the gift of prophecy to prove to people the existence of a spiritual world, a world beyond death—that perhaps his visions were God's way of drawing attention to the unknown. Comforted by this understanding, Joseph took on the role of messenger with a calmer conscience.

Fulfilling Destiny

In the 1960s and 1970s the subject of psychic phenomena was not widely discussed or accepted. There was general suspicion and dread of psychics. Fearing what they did not understand, individuals often labeled them charlatans.

As his success grew, Joseph was challenged more frequently and often harassed. The harassment extended to his family as well. One night Joseph and his family were awakened by sounds coming from outside—ugly menacing voices shouting and swearing. Looking out the window, he saw that a crowd had gathered in front of his house, pounded a cross into the ground, and set it afire. His wife Helen screamed when she saw it, fearing for her children, who awoke when they heard her cry.

The following morning Joseph discovered that not only had the vandals burned the cross but they had stolen the license plate from his car. While driving to work and unaware of the missing license plate, he was pulled over by a police officer. When the officer asked about his license plate, Joseph got out of the car and discovered the plate was missing. He related to the officer the previous evening's incident, but the officer wasn't buying it. A story that bizarre couldn't be true. He ticketed Joseph and advised him to tell it to the judge, which he proceeded to do. Fortunately for Joseph, the judge was interested in paranormal phenomena. When Joseph explained that he worked in parapsychology, the judge dismissed all charges.

Still the harassment continued. When his children walked to school or played outside, the neighborhood children at times tormented them. Warned by their parents to keep away from the DeLouises, their classmates taunted and teased them.

Joseph received anonymous phone calls blaming him for the events he foresaw and implying that he caused them to happen. Others accused him of doing "the work of the devil." Despite the contempt and ridicule, Joseph feverishly threw himself into his work. His psychic practice grew steadily and with it, more frequent appearances on radio programs.

Joseph knew people were wary of his ability to see into the future and to predict events that had not yet happened. As an ordained minister of the Independent Spiritualist Church, he performed exorcisms to cleanse houses of evil entities. He realized that many would find fault with that as well. Even so, when in the fall of 1971 he was asked to perform an exorcism on television, he accepted. Chicago's local NBC television station broadcast a special live segment of Reverends Joseph DeLouise and William Derl-Davis ridding a house on the northwest side of Chicago of lingering spirits.

The house was a two-flat purchased by Edwin and Marsha Becker in 1970. Shortly after moving in, they heard doors opening and closing by themselves, repeatedly found the phone off the hook, discovered keys bent out of shape, and heard footsteps and voices at all hours of day and night. When approached, Joseph agreed to perform an exorcism in the hope of clearing the home of what he believed were the spirits of a man and woman filled with bitterness. He enlisted Reverend Derl-Davis from the United Kingdom to assist him. Leading news reporter Carole Simpson was assigned to cover the story, narrating the ritual for the viewing audience.[8] A truncated version of the exorcism can be found at www.youtube.com/watch?v=y-6j3s65kC8.

Years later, at the encouragement of his granddaughter, Edwin Becker wrote *True Haunting*, an Amazon bestseller book about these paranormal experiences. He dedicated the book to Joseph, the only person who stepped forward to help them. Becker's book later became the basis for the episode entitled "The Tenants" on the television program, *Paranormal Witness*.

Joseph understood that people feared the unknown, especially death. They were eager to believe in a life beyond, but they needed proof—something he could provide them through his psychic powers. Each time one of his predictions materialized, he hoped it would help people to realize there is more to this life than is known; there exists an unseen spiritual side.

Those who met Joseph were attracted to him, wanting to draw upon his positive energy. Many who came to his office were happy, while others were sad. Joseph just as readily accepted those who were down in the dumps; he felt they were the ones most in need of his help. Some clients came to see Joseph after the loss of a loved one or some other tragic event. Listening in sympathy, Joseph would console and counsel the grief-stricken in their search for peace, advising them to keep in mind, "There are times in our lives when things happen from which we think we will never recover. What's important is how we come back from those events."

Throughout his long career, Joseph counseled several thousands of people from all walks of life—doctors, lawyers, nuns, police officers, millionaires, the poor, movie stars, radio and television personalities, teachers, parents and grandparents, stockbrokers, and politicians. Rich or poor, their lot in life wasn't important to Joseph; nor was their nationality or career of concern to him. He treated them all equally. Having come from a meager background and having achieved success, he was happy to help others to become successful.

Some clients sought help to drive "the voices" out of their heads after dabbling in black magic on the Ouija; unknowingly they had invited in a spirit that took possession of their minds and now controlled their thoughts and actions. A few psychiatrists sent Joseph patients whom they were unable to reach. Several medical doctors became converts and ended up as clients.

By now Joseph was getting attention, both when he was right and, more often, when he wasn't. The media were eager to pounce on a spectacular story that would provide interesting coverage. Some even preferred negative news, since a psychic's prediction that turned out to be wrong gave them an opportunity to say, "See, no one can glimpse the future." Disregarding his critics, Joseph knowingly ran the risk of criticism and ridicule and continued to publicize his predictions.

At first, his psychic talent didn't bring him monetary success. When he gave readings at his beauty shop, he often received only a quarter or half-dollar tip in exchange for his advice. Later, he opened an office he called Mind Unlimited where he charged twenty-five dollars per hour for readings. He raised his rate to thirty-five dollars an hour in the 1980s and fifty dollars, or according to a person's ability to pay, in the 1990s, increasing his fee to $75 an hour only in later years. Those who sought stock advice were charged a higher rate—sixty dollars an hour, later increased to ninety-five dollars for a forty-five-minute financial forecast. Numerous telephone calls were conducted free of charge. I was present when several such calls came in and observed that Joseph could not refuse anyone.

Wealth was not a part of Joseph's agenda. Accumulating money was not his motivation, even if at times he would have liked it to be. Although he could make money for other people, he found that he himself was unable to benefit from foreknowledge of the stock exchange. When he tried to make money for himself, something always interfered. It seemed that when he was personally involved with his forecasts, they didn't work.

Joseph was instead rewarded in spiritual riches. Each message from a deceased loved one or prophecy of a future event helped people realize that there was more to their existence than they had been aware. His predictions encouraged others to consider that we are more than our minds and bodies; we are spiritual beings as well. In Joseph's eyes, this was the way he could best fulfill his destiny.

MONEY TALKS TO JOSEPH

On July 3, 1971, while a guest on Al Park's financial radio program broadcast from Chicago on WCIU, Joseph picked ten stocks that he saw rising. A week and a half later, there was a market correction and nine out of the ten stocks rose. Parks validated the prediction on September 3, 1971 when Joseph next appeared on his program.

Throughout 1972, Joseph spoke on other radio programs, saying he saw the price of gold doubling and the Dow Jones Industrial average rising above 1000, both of which came about. In later interviews he told of seeing gold skyrocketing and the market plunging below 750.

When his predictions correctly materialized, *The Wall Street Journal* took notice and wrote in March 1973 article about how Joe DeLouise, a Chicago hairdresser who hardly ever reads the business pages, gives his psychic impressions of stocks to hundreds of stock brokers.

Others took notice as well. The Security and Exchange Commission (SEC), which oversees this country's stock market, strongly suggested to Joseph that he stop commenting on stocks, bonds, the Dow Jones average and the price of gold.

Joseph hired lawyers who argued that Joseph is not a financial consultant and only gives his feeling, good or bad, on his psychic impressions, which is his constitutional right.

The SEC disagreed, citing a 1940s Act. They threatened that Joseph may face prosecution — fined $10,000, given two years in jail, or both. They told him if he mentioned anything about stocks or the Dow Jones average when lecturing or while being interviewed, he would be violating that Act.

Joseph countered, saying he receives his impressions mentally and spiritually, and is upfront in telling people he is not a financial advisor.

Joseph continued giving his psychic impressions on stocks and the economy. It was only years later in the 1980s that Joseph decided to become a Registered Investment Adviser, passing the exam on the first try.

Author's note: This wasn't the only time that Joseph was threatened by those in authority. He told me the story of how in 1968 he was working in his beauty salon when two police officers barged in, handcuffed him and took him off to jail. The reason they gave? "For being a psychic."

Word had gotten around about the psychic readings that Joseph gave while he styled his clients' hair. At that time it was against the law to give psychic readings.

Joseph hired lawyers, fought the law and won. His actions opened the door, allowing psychics to legally practice their trade.

During the years that followed Joseph continued to speak of the market. In the 1980's, financial pundits for publications such as *Reuter's News Service, The Wall Street Journal, The Daily Herald Business section,* the *Chicago Sun-Times Business News* and the *Chicago Tribune* printed articles on Joseph DeLouise's amazing stock market predictions.

In June 1986, *PM Magazine,* a nationally syndicated television program broadcast a special segment featuring Joseph live from the floor of the Chicago Board of Trade. The program showed Joseph as he walked the floor while observing the rapidly changing numbers.

He spoke with traders, questioning them on how they made their buy/sell decisions, and, later in the program explained how he "psychically" reads the market.[10]

On July 6, 1987, while a guest on the Terry Savage financial television show *Money Talks,* Joseph advised people who had been in the five-year bull market to get out because he saw a drop of 750 to 950 points. He said he told his clients to start buying gold and silver futures, foreseeing their value would go up while the market would go down.

Over the next few weeks he repeated this same warning while giving radio and television interviews. On July 12, 1987, on Chicago's WGN radio station, Joseph warned, "The market will rise a bit more and then go straight down, settling in the Dow Jones Industrial Range of 1,400 to 1,500 until the following March."

On October 11 of that same year, he repeated the warning in an interview with Mildred Freese of the *Milwaukee Journal,* telling her the Dow would go to 2,780 and immediately down 1,200 points. The following Monday, October 19, 1987, the stock market crashed, a day infamously known as "Black Monday."

THE SHARON TATE MURDERS

A psychic detective is someone who investigates crimes using paranormal abilities such as postcognition (the paranormal perception of the past), psychometry (information psychically gained from objects), telepathy (transference of information from one mind to another), dowsing (the ancient art of seeking information or unseen objects) and remote viewing (to describe or give details about a target that is inaccessible to normal senses due to distance, time, or shielding).

In murder cases, psychic detectives may often claim to communicate with the spirits of the murder victims.

Brad Steiger, author of the book *Psychic City Chicago,* interviewed Joseph for an article in the August 1970 issue of the *National Tattler* titled "Joseph DeLouise: Psychic Detective." In it, he wrote about Joseph and his remarkable psychic impressions of the Sharon Tate murder case.

Indeed the Tate murders, carried out by members of the Charles Manson cult, were arguably the most compelling and disturbing case that Joseph ever worked on. He proved to be eerily accurate in his predictions, giving a California *Long Beach Press-Telegram* reporter details that weren't uncovered by police until much later.

Joseph's involvement began in mid-August 1969, when longtime friend Chris Harris, head of a public relations firm in California, phoned and was barely able to contain himself. He explained that the Sharon Tate murders, which had taken place a few days earlier on August 9, 1969 were all over the news. He'd just hung up with his friend, Mary Neiswender—staff writer for the Long Beach *Independent Press-Telegram*—who had already interviewed internationally known psychic Peter Hurkos about them. Chris had informed Mary that he knew of a Chicago psychic who was as good as Hurkos and who had correctly predicted the Kennedy-Kopechne drowning incident. Chris added, "Joseph, when I told her about you she said she'd like to get your impressions of the Tate tragedy." Chris's voice grew louder, "Can you fly out here and meet with us, Joseph? How quickly can you get here?" By now, he was practically shouting with excitement.

Joseph quietly told Chris that it wasn't necessary for him to come to California to pick up impressions on the case. He said he would relax, clear his mind, and see what came through, then call him back. Chris agreed but, before hanging up, he urged Joseph to hurry.

Since it was almost closing time, Joseph locked up the beauty shop and sat in the back room. His visions had been coming on a regular basis now, so he had brought one of his crystal balls to keep at work. As he gazed into the crystal, the horrors of that fateful night came through with startling clarity. The changing scenes, however, lacked continuity. There was no logical order to their presentation.

As we later talked of this event, Joseph told me that at first a hand appeared holding a knife that dripped blood. The scene quickly changed, and three figures came into view, their faces hidden by hoods. In the center of the hoods just above the eye slits was a white emblem that Joseph felt was a symbol for a gang. The physical characteristics of two men emerged. One had dark blond hair that framed his face and a jagged scar across the width of one cheek. The second man had a darker complexion and dark hair. Next, the word *Texas* flashed in Joseph's mind, giving him the impression that one of the murderers was from Texas or that he might be in Texas.

The scene changed again, and a string of unrelated images came into view—a woman holding a cat, a truck, auto parts strewn on the ground. The vision dissolved before coming to a sudden halt. This vision was unlike any other Joseph had received. The images had come through in bits and pieces; there was no order, the scenes lacked coherence. Similar to the Indianapolis plane crash where the meaning of the number *330* was unclear, the clues in this case were also cloudy. After fitting the symbols and impressions in order as best he could, Joseph called Chris, who then called Neiswender. Minutes later, Neiswender phoned Joseph. Her story of the psychic impressions of both Joseph and Hurkos was published in the *Independent-Press Telegram* on August 21, 1969, two weeks after the murders.

Following is an excerpt of the article that pertains to Joseph:

> The yet unsolved murder of movie star Sharon Tate and four others in her Benedict Canyon home was the work of "thrill killers," a nationally known Chicago psychic claims.

Joseph DeLouise, who predicted the collapse of a bridge in West Virginia and its subsequent loss of lives three weeks before the event actually happened, said today in an exclusive interview that "vibrations" coming to him 2,000 miles away were "very strong."

"This was a thrill murder... their joy was killing, so it didn't matter if they killed five... ten, or fifteen. The more they killed, the more joy they received."

"And... they have no conscience. They don't feel sorry about it; they're excited about it...

"Three people," he says, "committed the crime which has baffled the greatest detective force ever put on a case in Los Angeles...."[11]

The article included more information:

- "Joseph described one of the murderers as shorter than the other, saying he was more the Mediterranean type with dark hair."

- "He said the other weighs 160 pounds, has somewhat darkish blonde hair, long, with probably a wave in it."

- "One of the suspects could be in Texas...

- The three murderers were "friends" of the murdered people, but "not close friends... And drugs were involved...

- "One of the killers," the Italian-born seer says, "was a silent type, unusual voice—an introvert, with a scar on his face—like a piece of jagged glass had been pushed into it."

- "It will be almost impossible to bring these people to trial. There are no witnesses. But I think they will be caught."

- "One" he says, "will be freed, the other two 'tied up' in court but never really prosecuted for the crime...."[12]

Four months later, Mary Neiswender wrote a second article, a follow-up to the first, published in the *Independent Press-Telegram* on December 3, 1969. An excerpt follows:

Psychic Described Tate 'Thrill Killers'

Two weeks after the slaughter of actress Sharon Tate and four of her jet-set friends, Chicago hairdresser-psychic Joseph DeLouise gave his impressions of the killers. His comments, published August 21 in the *Independent Press-Telegram,* almost paralleled police disclosures...

DeLouise said, at that time, three people had committed the crime and went further to describe the suspects:

"One weighs 180 pounds with darkish blonde hair, long, with probably a wave in it." [Charles "Tex" Watson weighs 156 pounds, is six feet two, and has light brown hair.] "The other is shorter with dark hair—probably a Mediterranean type...." [Charles Manson is five feet seven inches, weighs 140 pounds, and has dark brown hair and brown eyes.]

Then DeLouise pinpointed a state: "One of the suspects could be in Texas... he could have been in an institution in Texas, either a mental or drug institution, or in jail...." [Charles "Tex" Watson was arrested for the Tate murders in Texas. Back in California after his arrest, Watson suffered acute paranoia and regressed to a fetal state. He remained silent and stopped eating, eventually dropping fifty-five pounds. He was placed in Atascadero State Hospital for a ninety-day observation period to determine if he was able to stand trial.]

The psychic pinpointed a date also: "September 14 and 15—that's the date when there will be a break in the case. I feel good about that."

That's the date, say police authorities in Inyo County, when they first "ran into" the hippie cult that was finally held responsible by police for the slayings.

One of the suspects could be a "mechanic," DeLouise said four months ago. The hippie colony existed on profits from stolen cars—they would steal Volkswagens and convert them into dune buggies and sell them....[13]

"The three murderers were 'friends' of the murdered people, but not 'close friends.' [Watson had been to the house on at least one other occasion.]

"Drugs were involved...." [The Manson family was heavily into drugs.]

Now that the three suspects have been arrested in the case, DeLouise said his impressions continue.

"I get the impression of money—money that wasn't exchanged. There was something about movies—I don't know if they were fooling around with stag movies. There's a linkup between money and black magic and movies.... Somebody was cheated out of some money, and they wanted to get even... I get the word 'gold-diggers.'"

He says he feels only three are involved in the actual Tate murders. He doesn't feel that five more will be indicted, as police hope. "I feel maybe just two more—making it five in all ... the rest may be associated with the crime as witnesses but not participating."[14]

In early December, while under oath, Susan Atkins testified in front of the grand jury that she was in "love with the reflection" of Charles Manson and there was "no limit" to what she would do for him. She went on to describe the murders at the Tate estate and told how, after the murders, the "family" pulled off on a side street, stopping at a house to wash off their bloody clothes with a garden hose. After twenty minutes of deliberation, the grand jury returned murder indictments against Manson, Watson, Krenwinkel, Atkins, Kasabian, and Van Houten.

On December 9, 1970, Neiswender wrote a third piece about Joseph after he predicted that Leslie Van Houten's defense attorney, Ronald Hughes, who had been missing since November, would be found dead. An excerpt from the article follows:

Psychic Predicts Missing Manson Attorney Is Dead

Chicago psychic Joseph DeLouise, who "vibrated" two weeks after the Tate and LaBianca massacre murders, predicting the arrest of five "thrill killers" with unbelievable accuracy, today claimed the missing attorney in the sensational case is dead.

Today, DeLouise, a Chicago hairdresser and the father of six, again told of "impressions" in the case, which is now centered around the disappearance of Leslie Van Houton's defense attorney [Ronald Hughes]. He has been missing since Thanksgiving.

"Something happened to his left foot," DeLouise claims. "I'm getting something about a boot—or a high shoe—and receiving pain there. Then I received pain on my left side, like the man had a heart attack.

"I see a casket—the only thing I can get is that the man is dead....

"I feel he was with somebody—this is what I can't understand—why the person didn't turn up...."[15]

Hughes had gone on a camping trip to a remote area near Sespe Hot Springs in Ventura County, California, after Judge Charles Older ordered a ten-day recess in the Tate–LaBianca murder trial to allow attorneys time to prepare their final arguments. James Forsher and Lauren Elder, two friends who accompanied Hughes on the trip, told of heavy rains, which caused flash floods that mired their Volkswagen in the mud. Forsher and Elder hitchhiked their way out; Hughes decided he would stay until November 29. The rains continued and the area was evacuated. Hughes was last seen by three campers on the morning of November 28. They spoke with him briefly and later told investigators that Hughes was in an area away from floodwaters and appeared to be unharmed. When the court reconvened on November 30 and Hughes failed to appear, a search was ordered. However, due to continued rainfall, the search was not able to begin until two days later.]

Searchers from the Ventura Sheriff's station said that two escaped convicts were in the area and Hughes may have "run into" them.

"I know he didn't die instantly—I'm getting a period of five days, like he'd been lost for five days before he died."[16]

[Three months later, on March 29, 1971, two anglers in Ventura County discovered the badly decomposed body of Ronald Hughes under three feet of water, wedged between two boulders in a gorge.]

The Sharon Tate murder case remained in the press for nearly a year. While it brought Joseph much publicity, he would gladly have done without it since everything about the case—the killers' nonchalant attitude, their complete lack of remorse, their boastfulness of the deeds sickened him, as it did the public.

Events associated with the case continue to make news. Charles Manson appealed for parole and was denied twelve times, most recently in April 2012. He could be eligible again in 2027.

Charles "Tex" Watson has been denied parole fourteen times; his next hearing is in 2016. Patricia Krenwinkel has been denied parole thirteen times, most recently in 2011. Susan Atkins died in September 2009, at the age of sixty-one, after being denied parole thirteen times. Leslie Van Houten has been denied parole nineteen times and will be eligible again in 2018.

Linda Kasabian was granted immunity in exchange for testimony. Others who received sentences include Steve "Clem" Grogan, who was paroled in 1985; Lynette "Squeaky" Fromme, who was paroled in 2009; Bruce Davis, who has been recommended for parole; and Bobby Beausoleil, for whom parole has been denied several times.

THE ZODIAC KILLER

Zodiac was a serial killer who brought terror to the people of northern California in the late 1960s and early 1970s. On December 20, 1968, Zodiac attacked and killed two high school students, Betty Lou Jensen, age sixteen, and David Faraday, age seventeen, in Benicia, California. It was their first date. The young couple had planned to go to a concert at their high school but instead ended up eating at a restaurant and then stopping at around 10:15 p.m. to park at a local lovers' lane. A short time later, a car pulled up. A man got out and shot into Faraday's vehicle, shooting out the right rear window, the left rear and then the front left tires. Attempting to get away, the two teenagers rushed out the passenger door.

Jensen ran toward the road. Her body was found by the police about twenty-eight feet from the rear bumper. She had been shot five times along the right side of her back from the ribs to the pelvis. Faraday was killed by a single shot to the head. The police found his body with his feet at the rear wheel and his head pointing away from the front of the car, suggesting he was killed as he ran from the vehicle. A reward was offered by students of the victims' high school, but the killer was never found.

Six months later, on July 4, 1969, shortly after 12 a.m., two young lovers, Michael Mageau, age nineteen, and Darlene Ferrin, age twenty-two, were shot as they sat in Ferrin's car after stopping to park in the Blue Rock Springs Park in Vallejo, California. Just before midnight, a brown car pulled up alongside them, stayed there briefly, and then drove away. Ten minutes later the car pulled up behind Ferrin's car. The driver got out and walked up to the couple's car. He carried a flashlight and a 9mm Luger.

The killer shined the flashlight at the couple's eyes, blinding them. Thinking it was a police officer, Mageau reached for his driver's license. The man then fired five rounds through the window, first hitting Mageau in the face and body. Several bullets passed through Mageau, entering Ferrin's body. Mageau managed to crawl to the backseat and, as he did, another shot went through his knee. The attacker then fired at Ferrin, hitting her in each arm and then her back. The killer walked away, only to return when he heard moans coming from the victims. He shot each of them two more times before driving off. Still conscious, Mageau turned the car's blinkers on, stumbled out the passenger door, and collapsed on the pavement. From there, he saw the car pull out and drive off. Managing to catch a glimpse of the man, Mageau described him as short, about five feet eight inches, and extremely heavyset.

Other teenagers called the police, who called for an ambulance. Mageau was rushed into surgery and survived. Ferrin died in the ambulance on the way to the hospital.

On July 5, 1969, at 12:40 am, a man phoned the Vallejo Police Department to claim responsibility for the attack. The caller bragged that six months earlier he had murdered two others in Benicia, California.

On July 31, 1969, the *San Francisco Examiner, San Francisco Chronicle,* and *Vallejo Times-Herald* each received letters from a person claiming to be the murderer. Enclosed with each letter was one-third of a cryptogram, along with instructions to publish it on the front page of any issue by August 1.

The author expressed intimate knowledge of each murder and promised another killing spree if these demands were not met. Each letter was worded differently but stated the same facts and contained a crossed-circle design, which was to become Zodiac's signature. The letters were checked for fingerprints by the Vallejo and San Francisco police, but none were found.

The next attack came on September 27, 1969, about sixty miles northeast of San Francisco. Bryan Calvin Hartnell, age twenty, and Cecelia Ann Shepard, age twenty-two, were picnicking in a remote area at Lake Berryessa in Napa County. At twilight, they were approached by a man who was about six feet tall, dark haired, and heavyset. He was wearing a dark jacket, dark clothing, and sunglasses. Before he got closer to the couple, he stopped and put on a hood with clip-on sunglasses covering the eyeholes.

On his belt hung a long knife and an empty leather holster. As he approached the couple, he pointed a large pistol at them, saying he wanted their money and car keys. He said he was an escaped convict who had killed a prison guard and was going to Mexico. Hartnell quickly gave him his change and car keys.

The man then took some clothesline from his belt and ordered Shepard to tie up Hartnell. When she was done, the man tied up Shepard. He seemed nervous and told the couple he was going to have to stab them. Hartnell couldn't stand to see Shepard stabbed and told the man to stab him first.

The man stabbed Hartnell eight times with a double-edged, foot-long knife, then stabbed Shepard ten times. Leaving them for dead, the attacker walked to Hartnell's car and drew his crossed-circle insignia on the door, along with the dates of his Bay Area attacks.

A fisherman who heard the screams of Hartnell and Shepard alerted park rangers. By the time an ambulance reached the couple they were in critical condition. Shepard died two days later, on September 29. Hartnell recovered from his wounds.

The next incident attributed to Zodiac took place on the night of October 11, 1969. San Francisco cab driver Paul Stine picked up a passenger at the intersection of Mason and Geary Streets in Union Square. Stine reported to his dispatcher that he was taking his passenger to the corner of Washington and Maple streets in Presidio Heights. However, Stine never made it to Maple Street. Instead, the passenger shot him in the head one block west of Maple, at the corner of Washington and Cherry Streets.

On October 14, 1969, the *Chronicle* received another letter from Zodiac claiming responsibility for the murder. The return address on the envelope was the crossed-circle design. Enclosed with the letter was a swatch of Paul Stine's bloody shirt. The writer of the letter claimed to be the murderer of the taxi driver last night by Washington and Maple Streets, pointing out the enclosed blood-stained shirt as proof. In the letter he included a threat to kill school children as they exited a school bus; however, this threat was never carried out.

Zodiac's next letter was sent to the *Chronicle* in early November in an envelope with double the instruction "Please Rush to Editor." Inside was a greeting card and another lengthy cypher. This letter contained Zodiac's first claim to a body count, a number that rose steadily with each new mailing. However, no evidence suggests that Zodiac was responsible for any murders other than the six attributed to him.

In December 1969, Chris Harris spoke with Bud Kressin of the *Vallejo Times-Herald*, telling him that Chicago psychic Joseph DeLouise had recently begun receiving impressions on Zodiac. Kressin was familiar with Joseph and his psychic impressions given to the Los Angeles police in the Sharon Tate murder case. He wanted to know Joseph's impressions of Zodiac.

When Kressin called Joseph at his office in Chicago, Joseph asked him to hold while he went into a trance. Joseph was able to still his mind and slip into a trance in a matter of moments; he had recently learned that if a vision was slated, it wouldn't take long to appear. Several minutes went by. When Joseph got back on the phone, he told Kressin that he saw Zodiac as a man with dark brown hair who was about twenty-eight years old, stood around five feet eight inches tall, and weighed 135 to 145 pounds. Joseph also said he felt the killer would attempt to turn himself in and gave a date—January 4, 1970. His impression was that the killer was remorseful and seeking capture. He felt that Zodiac's July 5 call to the police bragging about what he had done was actually a plea for help.

After speaking with Joseph, Kressin wrote a four-column article that spread across the width of the front page of the Sunday, January 4, 1970, *Vallejo-Times Herald.*

The article read:

Zodiac May Give Up Today, Seer Says

Zodiac might give himself up today. Or begin a series of steps leading to his surrender.

A Chicago hairdresser, whose amazing psychic powers have given him an uncanny ability to see into the future, told the *Times-Herald* in an exclusive interview by long-distance telephone that he believes a major break in the Zodiac case involving the psychotic murders of five persons in the Bay Area—three of them here—may well occur today, January 4.

Joseph DeLouise, a forty-one-year-old seer whose predictions have astonished authorities for two years, said he has received extrasensory impressions for the last three or four days that murder no longer holds a thrill for Zodiac and that he may make a sincere effort to surrender himself today.

"I keep getting impressions that Zodiac wants to turn himself in…that he wants help," DeLouise said. "The thrill of what he did is now over, and he wants peace of mind. I feel he doesn't want to kill again."

The Chicago mystic said the "vibrations" coming to him from 2,000 miles away have convinced him that the elusive slayer at least will make preliminary arrangements to give himself up.

"He won't just walk in," DeLouise said. "He will want to complicate matters by turning himself in. He knows it will be a three-ring circus type of thing when he surrenders, but if he can find a channel to turn himself in—someone who understands the mystic side of his life—he will give himself up."

DeLouise said that person might be Melvin Belli, the San Francisco attorney who two or three weeks ago received a letter from Zodiac containing a plea for help, or someone like himself who can establish a telepathic contact with him and create a sympathetic understanding of his psyche. "I think Zodiac has no one who really understands him," DeLouise said.[17]

For two weeks Joseph continued to receive the impression that the killer wanted to turn himself in. Consequently, Joseph traveled to the Bay Area at his own expense to help Zodiac find "peace of mind." Arriving in San Francisco on January 20, 1970, he was met by Harris, and together they drove to the Vallejo Police Department, where officers took them to the site of the Jensen-Faraday murders. Next they visited Napa law officials, who gave Joseph details of the Lake Berryessa slaying.

Joseph gave the police further impressions he received about the killer. He said he saw the man was lonely, involved with horses and a white dog, and that he hated the police. He explained he had picked up the impression of two men involved in the murders and that these two knew each other well. One was strong, the other weak. Joseph felt the weak one suffered from an emotional illness. He saw that the stronger of the two men had helped the weaker one to develop and take on the persona of Zodiac.

Joseph didn't believe that Zodiac had murdered all the victims attributed to him. His psychic insight told him the original Zodiac had carried out two of the crimes and then mentioned to the other man his desire to confess. This led to an altercation between them and ended with the stronger man killing the original Zodiac. Joseph felt that after killing the original Zodiac, the second man took over and went on to commit more murders. He also felt that Zodiac would never be caught [and he never was].

On January 21, Joseph was interviewed by Bud Kressin of the *Vallejo Times-Herald*. The resulting article included a photograph of Joseph speaking with Kressin, who was seated at a typewriter. Beneath the photograph was the headline "DeLouise Arrives on Coast," while above it was a reprint of the above mentioned article, "Zodiac May Give up Today, Seer Says."

In the book, *Zodiac,* published in 1986 by St. Martin's Press, author Robert Graysmith described Joseph's involvement in the case and in *Zodiac Unmasked: The Identity of America's Most Elusive Serial Killer Revealed,* published by the Penguin Group in 2007, Graysmith told of how after twenty years Joseph was still receiving psychic impressions of Zodiac. In the section he dated October 1987, Graysmith wrote that Joseph said he'd had a second vision in which he saw Zodiac was either a Scorpio or an Aquarian since he kept receiving the figures 11-2 and 2-11, and, was living near Berkley.

Joseph went on to tell of two phone calls he had received from the San Francisco area. The first was from a woman who believed her boyfriend was the killer. At the time, Joseph saw danger around her. A second call came a few weeks later from a man who spoke only two words: "I'm back."

Although the woman had promised Joseph she would call him back, she did not, which led him to believe she was dead.

Joseph felt the man was troubled and that he might reach out and call him. Zodiac didn't call, but eerily, on October 28, 1987, two letters were mailed from a San Francisco mailbox to area newspapers. One to the *Chronicle,* the other to the *Vallejo Times-Herald.* Both letters bore Zodiac's insignia.

This case was especially perturbing to Joseph. It left him feeling incomplete— as if something had been left undone. When speaking of it to me, he said that he had failed; that on looking back, he felt he should have stayed in California longer and continued trying to get through to Zodiac. He believed that if he had been able to reach him, he might have been able to help Zodiac put an end to the killings.

Decades later, in the 1990s, a woman from the San Francisco area contacted Joseph, telling him she believed her late husband was the Zodiac Killer. She was convinced he was Zodiac but, afraid of him, had waited to say anything until after his death.

Joseph asked if she still had anything that belonged to the man. The woman claimed she had some articles of clothing, including a hat with leather trim. Joseph asked her to send the hat to him and he would have it tested for DNA.

One of Joseph's many connections to the Chicago police force arranged to have a DNA test conducted. However, there wasn't sufficient DNA on the hat, so the lab test proved inconclusive.

BURIED ALIVE

⸻

I n November 1978, Joseph received an urgent phone call from Ray Garner, head of a Joplin, Missouri, K9 Search and Rescue unit, requesting his help immediately. Garner said that three men were working in the basement of the Joplin Connor Hotel when the building, which was slated to be demolished, came crashing down on them. Rescuers had spent three days using heavy earth-moving equipment in an attempt to find survivors.

Garner, together with his German shepherd, Sir Joel, had helped with the search for survivors to no avail. While discussing where to refocus their search efforts, they acquired Joseph's phone number from radio station KSLQ in St. Louis, where Joseph had taken part recently in a weekly talk show.

Joseph asked Garner to describe the scene. He then asked Garner to hold on a few minutes while he centered his mind. When he returned to the phone, Joseph told Garner exactly where to find the three people who were trapped. They were within close proximity of each other in the upper northeast corner of the collapsed building.

Garner and other rescuers rushed to the place Joseph had identified. When Garner's dog kept sniffing at the same spot, they began to dig. They stopped when Garner heard someone shout. Five hours later, they pulled Alfred "Butch" Summers from beneath the rubble where he was trapped in an air pocket that had kept him alive for eighty-two hours.

After Summers was rescued, Garner again called Joseph, who focused his mind as before. This time Joseph saw that two other workers were alive but unconscious. He told Garner they wouldn't last long so immediate action was required. Twenty-four hours later a second man was extricated from the rubble, then the third. Unfortunately, both were dead.

A news release about Joseph's role in the event, broadcast on November 14, 1978, over St. Louis radio station KSLQ appears below:

```
KSLQ

WITH HOTEL COLLAPSE

    (ST. LOUIS) -- A PROFESSIONAL PSYCHIC FROM CHICAGO SAYS HE WAS ASKED
TO HELP IN THE SEARCH FOR THREE WORKERS MISSING IN THE RUBBLE OF A
COLLAPSED HOTEL IN JOPLIN, MISSOURI, AND WAS ABLE TO VISUALIZE WHERE
THE MEN ARE AND THAT ALL THREE ARE ALIVE.
    ONE OF THE WORKERS WAS PULLED FROM THE DEBRIS ALIVE THIS EVENING AND
THE SEARCH CONTINUES FOR THE OTHER TWO.
    IN A LONG DISTANCE TELEPHONE INTERVIEW TODAY, JOSPH DELOUISE OF
CHICAGO SAYS HE GOT A CALL YESTERDAY FROM RAYMOND GARNER OF
FLORISSANT, WHO WAS ON HIS WAY WITH HIS GERMAN SHEPHERD TO HELP THE
SEARCHERS. GARNER, THE HEAD OF LAW ENFORCEMENT K-9 SEARCH AND RESCUE
INCORPORATED, WAS PUT IN TOUCH WITH DELOUISE BY RADIO STATION K-S-L-Q
IN ST. LOUIS, WHERE THE PSYCHIC TAKES PART IN A WEEKY TALK SHOW.
    DELOUISE SAYS GARNER ASKED HIM TO MEDITATE AND TELL HIM WHERE THE
SEARCH SHOULD CONCENTRATE. IN HIS OWN WORDS, THE PSYCHIC SAYS, ''I
TOLD HIM TO LAY OUT A PLAN OF THE BUILDING AND TO SEARCH THE UPPER
LEFT HAND SIDE. I TOLD HIM HE WOULD FIND THREE BODIES ALIVE IF HE DID
IT RIGHT AWAY.''
    DELOUISE SAYS WHEN GARNER CALLED HIM THIS AFTERNOON TO SAY HE HAD
BEEN RIGHT, HE TOLD GARNER TO GET INTO THE BUILDING FROM UNDERNEATH
THE STREET TO SEARCH FOR THE OTHER MEN.
03:52PCS   11-14-78
```

Figure 2. Broadcast transcription from St. Louis radio station KSLQ, November 14, 1978.

PART II
THE MAKING OF A PSYCHIC

A Life Uncommon

J oseph was born in Gibellina, Sicily, a small village nestled among the mountains of southern Italy. The townspeople of Gibellina held family and church in the highest esteem and would spend days keeping jealous watch over their families and their property, so much so that it was dangerous to trespass against either one.

Although their faith was strong, the people of Gibellina feared having a curse put on them, and so dared not even glance at anyone said to have the "evil eye." The villagers went out of their way to avoid such individuals, giving them ample distance. If a vindictive member of the community succeeded in putting a hex on a neighbor, it was customary to call on a mystic to cleanse the person's house or purge the demon thought to possess them. Mystics rid the citizenry of malevolent spells and drove away evil spirits.

Villagers bragged about having a resident mystic. If a town did not have one, the townspeople would do whatever was necessary to lure a mystic from a nearby village. Gibellina was fortunate, for it had Joseph "Papa" Plaia, a healer and psychic who was both respected and revered. Not only did he practice in the town of Gibellina, he also traveled the nearby hills to heal men, women, and children.

Joseph Plaia was young Joseph's maternal grandfather. Joseph's mother, Caterina, remembered people coming to the house at all hours, imploring her father to heal a family member who had taken ill. When performing a healing, her father would stand above the ailing person, uttering words so softly that others couldn't discern what he was saying. As he spoke, his hands hovered above the affected area, moving in circular motions, stopping only when he felt the cure had taken hold.

The villagers spoke reverently of the esteemed Joseph Plaia, marveling at the things he could do. Not only did Joseph Plaia restore people's health, he was also an animal whisperer, communicating telepathically with farm animals to cure them of disease. A number of people swore they had heard the words he spoke during his healings and were certain they came from an old, long-forgotten language.

Joseph's mother, a devoutly religious person, would say a special prayer each day to St. Joseph, her patron saint. Having inherited some psychic ability from her father, Caterina was known for her ability to see the future in dreams.

Joseph's mother and his father, Mike DeLouise, were betrothed at birth. Marrying young, they lived in the house where Caterina had spent most of her childhood. After their marriage, Papa Plaia moved to America and gave Caterina the family house as a wedding gift. Mike's own father gave him a large piece of land to farm. The soil was fertile and the crops abundant. Life in Gibellina was good for them.

Their first son, Joseph's older brother Nick, was born a year after Mike and Caterina married. Four years passed before Caterina gave birth, on November 10, 1927, to a second son, Joseph.

Her first delivery had been easy, but Joseph's birth turned out to be extremely difficult. Caterina had been forewarned of this. Shortly before Joseph's birth, She was walking along a garden path when a large snake suddenly slithered out of the bushes, stopped in front of her and coiled itself, hissing its threat. Frightened, Caterina ran away. Although she ran from the snake, she knew running from the warning was not possible. Being frightened by a snake during pregnancy portended a difficult birth—a sign Caterina took seriously.

Caterina expected to have a prolonged labor, but never did she think the birth would be life-threatening. The mysterious events surrounding Joseph's birth clearly indicated to Caterina that her new-born son would be destined to a life of service to others, a fate dictated by none other than St. Joseph, her patron saint. With the first breath he drew, Joseph's future was sealed.

Each time she repeated the story to family members, Joseph sensed she was speaking directly to him, as if he were the only one in the room. Here is the story as Caterina told it:

> "Oh, Joseph, the pain—for so long such pain you gave me. All that night and throughout the next day, you refused to be born. Then night came again and with it more pain, but no baby. The midwife, who had delivered most of the babies in Gibellina—even she could do no more. She avoided looking into my eyes, afraid that I would see the fear of death in hers. We were both sure that death lay ahead.
>
> "The second night passed slowly, and with each hour I grew weaker. Toward morning, with the last of my breath I closed my eyes

and kissed the medallion of St. Joseph that I always wore around my neck. I prayed for him to take me but to let my baby live."

With those words, Caterina would stop and look solemnly at Joseph before going on.

"Closing my eyes in prayer, I pleaded and promised St. Joseph if he let you live I would have twelve candles lighted to honor him. When I opened my eyes, I saw St. Joseph standing next to me. His presence calmed me. His eyes held assurance that things would be all right and soon after, you, my precious son, were born into this world.

"Later, the midwife told everyone in the village it was no wonder I was in such pain. Never before had she delivered a baby so big—more than twelve pounds were you.

"But I was close to death, so weak I could hardly move. I whispered to my sister, who had come to help, to bring me twelve candles. She promised, but then did not. She feared that if she brought them I would die.

"Two weeks passed. During that time I grew stronger, but you, Joseph, each day you lost weight and grew weaker. I watched as life faded from you. I prayed fervently to God, asking him to let you live.

"I was eager for you to be baptized lest you should slip away. While I was dressing you for the ritual, the room suddenly grew cool—a sign that a spirit was present. I turned and saw St. Joseph standing very close by, watching the two of us. I knew he had come for you, my precious Joseph."

Joseph told me that each time his mother reached this place in the story, tears came to her eyes. It mattered not how many years had passed, or how often she spoke of it. So affected was she by the event that each time she repeated the account, she relived the fear of nearly losing him.

Trembling, Caterina continued:

"As St. Joseph stepped closer and reached out to take you, I picked you up in my arms and held you close. Pleading and crying, I beseeched that he not take you. I begged his forgiveness for not light-ing the candles and gave him my word that I would serve him the rest of my life. With that, St. Joseph slowly backed away. As he faded from view, in my mind I heard him say that it was not the candles or the begging, nor even my promise that had saved you. He told me your life had been spared because your destiny was to serve him."

Thus it was that Joseph's mother was certain his future was to serve St. Joseph. Throughout her life, Caterina remained unwavering in her staunch belief of the spiritual experience she'd had. Never once did Joseph doubt his mother's conviction regarding the appearance of St. Joseph. A devout Catholic, Caterina would have found it inconceivable—nothing short of a sin—to state a falsehood against any saint, let alone her patron saint.

So powerful was her experience that Caterina faithfully kept her promise. Each year thereafter, on the nineteenth day of March, she honored her patron saint on the day the church designated as the Feast of St. Joseph. She paid homage to St. Joseph by opening her home to anyone who wished to eat at her table. Caterina welcomed all who wished to partake of the abundance of pasta dishes and sweets she had prepared in honor of her patron saint, turning no one away. If a pasta dish began to run low, she would hurry to the kitchen to make more.

Soon there were further signs. Now healthy and nearly two months old, Joseph slept in a bedroom off the kitchen. As Caterina prepared the evening meal, a loud thud came from his room. Thinking the worst, the young mother rushed to check on her child. As she looked down at her son asleep in the crib, Caterina saw a sign that startled her so greatly she immediately fell to her knees: a beam of light spread out like a halo surrounding Joseph's head. Caterina gasped, crossed herself, and began to pray. As she prayed, she looked up toward heaven.

It was then that she spotted the hole in the roof and the light streaming in. Following the beam of light, her eyes found a second hole, this one in the floor very close to the head of the tiny crib. Caterina hurried from the room and ran to the earthen cellar. The beam of light shone on a spot in the cellar where a meteor had buried itself in the ground. Ecstatic, Caterina dug it up, thinking this surely must be an omen, a sign straight from heaven that her son was to live a special life. For the rest of her life she kept the meteor safe under her protection. She made certain to keep Joseph safe under her protection as well.

Joseph's father often took his son Nick to the farm to help him tend the crops. Rarely did Caterina allow him to take Joseph. Joseph said he could only remember a few times when, against his mother's will, his father would sit him on the family's donkey and take him along while he gathered crops to sell at the village market.

Caterina believed Joseph to be fragile. Fretting over him, she kept him close. Joseph spent his days accompanying his mother as she cooked and cleaned. In the afternoons as they rested from the heat, Caterina would tell him stories of the wonderful things done by her father, Papa Plaia.

She loved her father dearly and longed to be with him in America. Many times Caterina would close her eyes and dreamily say, "Oh, Joseph, I can't wait until we join your grandfather in Chicago. When we do, you will see that what I say about him is true. Papa will teach you the things you need to know. Just you wait. You will see."

Joseph's clairvoyance was apparent early. At the tender age of three, he was able to find lost items. Family members and neighbors would stop by the house to ask him where they could find the things they'd misplaced. Little Joseph would close his eyes and, upon opening them, tell the people where to look.

Life in Gibellina was good. Joseph basked and played in the warmth of the days. Both the boy and the farm flourished under the bountiful Sicilian sun.

Then suddenly the weather, which had always blessed the crops with near-perfect rainfall, turned bad. Little rain fell throughout the rainy season. Months went by with no rain in sight. The same sun that had brought prosperity to the family now brought poverty, as it dried the ground, causing crops to fail.

Joseph's mother scrimped and pinched pennies in a desperate attempt to save money for the family's passage to America, where her beloved father awaited them. Things were looking bleak when one day a miracle happened—one that involved Joseph. Caterina had always believed that Joseph was special, but never did she dream that her young son would be the one to come to the family's rescue.

Early Psychic Events

⁍━━━━⁌

Joseph had his first psychic experience a few months shy of his fifth birthday. Being so young, Joseph depended on what his mother said, rather than on his own recall of the incident. One story she loved to tell began on a day when Mike let Joseph ride the family's donkey. First, Mike fitted the donkey with two large baskets, which were slung together so that each hung on one side of the animal. He then sat Joseph atop the donkey and took him to the farm, where Mike proceeded to collect produce that had survived the drought. Joseph liked riding on the donkey, and he enjoyed playing at the farm.

There, fruit trees grew alongside the rows of vegetables. Joseph would run among the trees, circling them until he tired. Weary from his exercise, he lay down to rest in the shade and listen to the birds sing as they flew from limb to limb high above him.

After his rest, it was Joseph's habit to pick up a stick and march around the grove. He'd march boldly, as if he were there to inspect the property. This always brought a smile to his father's face. On this particular day, Joseph was drawn to one of the smaller trees that bordered the farm. As he approached it, he suddenly felt cold in spite of the heat from the sun. Joseph sensed a spirit was nearby. Other than stopping short, he gave little attention to its presence. In Gibellina ghosts and spirits were common, a natural part of life. Even at his young age, he had often heard his family speak of them.

Standing beside the tree, Joseph had the impression that he should dig. Without hesitation, he crouched to the ground, shoved a stick into the earth, and began digging. The earth beneath the tree was soft, not hardened from lack of rain. Joseph dug until he tired.

Leaning back on his heels to rest, he glanced to one side and found he was staring straight at a pair of dusty, black boots. A long heavy coat swept the top of them. Someone was standing right next to him, and it wasn't his father! Joseph's eyes traveled upward until he was looking into the face of a man he'd never before seen. Although the man had shocks of long white hair sticking out from beneath his tall black hat, his face looked young. The man's eyes were clear blue, like his. When he looked at the hole Joseph had dug, the man's eyes danced with excitement. He seemed pleased. Smiling, he pointed to the hole and nodded his encouragement to keep digging.

Joseph went back to work, scooping out handful after handful of dirt. The deeper he dug, the stronger the feeling he should keep digging. When next he stopped to catch his breath, Joseph looked around and the man was gone.

Poking the stick deeper into the ground, Joseph heard a thud and saw a piece of burlap sticking out of the dirt. Running to get his father, Joseph dragged him to the hole, telling him about the man he had seen. When he told his father that a piece of cloth was sticking out of the ground, Mike dropped to his knees and began digging furiously.

Soon his fingers hit something hard, whereupon he loosened the object, pulled it from the hole, and stripped away the heavy burlap in which it was wrapped. Another piece of burlap was beneath the first. Unfolding it, he found an old, heavy box. Opening the lid, Mike was astonished to find that it contained jewels and several old gold coins. Mike quickly packed up the mule and raced home with Joseph and the box.

When Caterina heard what her son had found, she picked him up. Crying and laughing at the same time, she swung him in circles high above her head, praising him, calling him her hero, repeating that he had saved the family. Much later, she told Joseph that the man with the clear blue eyes and white hair was strangely reminiscent of her older brother who died in his late twenties, when she was a young girl.

[Upon hearing this part of the story, I remembered that an autoimmune disease or hormonal imbalance of the pituitary or thyroid causes some people to go prematurely gray by the age of twenty, which could have been the case with Caterina's brother.]

It was long rumored that a treasure was buried in Gibellina, but no one had been able to find it. Caterina told family members she should have expected that Joseph would be the one to unearth it, given his ability to locate lost objects.

After Joseph discovered the treasure, his mother was even more convinced he had a special gift. She began taking him to church and to people's homes to have him heal the sick. Years later, remembering those early days in Italy, Joseph confided in me that he would rather have been playing outside but instead went with his mother to these spots where he would place his hands on the sick, close his eyes, and say a prayer. "In Italy," he told me, "one learns to pray at an early age."

In the meantime, Joseph's father negotiated the sale of the family farm and successfully sold the coins and jewels. With the money he received, the family was able to book passage on a ship to America. Caterina willed the house to her sister and made the family ready for the long journey to be with her dear father, Papa Plaia, who would be waiting to embrace them.

PAPA PLAIA

The journey across the ocean in the summer of 1932 was long and arduous. Cramped quarters and slow passage made it even more difficult, but Caterina did not mind. No matter how rough the sea became, she felt as if the ship was floating on air. Frightened by the tossing waves, Joseph was somewhat consoled when he heard his mother whispering that the ship was magic for it was the vessel taking them to her father.

Papa Plaia was there to greet the family when they arrived in Chicago. Joseph watched his mother's smile widen and her eyes brighten before filling with tears at the sight of her beloved father. Joseph, who previously had only seen pictures of his grandfather, was completely awestruck. Papa Plaia stood strong and proud, presenting a commanding figure not easily ignored. As Joseph looked into his grandfather's clear blue eyes, he was sure they could see straight into his heart.

Papa Plaia had many lessons for Joseph. He cautioned him not to interfere in other people's business regardless of their thoughts or actions, telling him, "People have been given free will, and their progress depends on how they choose to work out their problems." He spoke of the importance of showing kindness and gratitude, of not seeking revenge.

He talked about karma, saying, "It is neither good nor bad, neither punishment nor reward; it's the result of the actions we take. In other words, the deeds of a soul create karmic experiences." He added that karma simply presents us with situations we *need* to experience. Papa looked at Joseph and smiled, then said, "Remember, Joseph, karma needn't last forever. We overcome it through forgiveness—forgiveness of self and forgiveness of others."

Papa patiently tutored Joseph. He told him there would be times when he'd keep the things he saw to himself to prevent bringing harm to him or to another. He said that sometimes a vision of the future could appear without warning, even when not meditating. "When this happens," Papa counseled, "just relax and don't fight it. Spirit brings us what is important, as needed."

He told Joseph to speak in a way that people could easily understand, without fancy words or complicated explanations, and to tie his advice to the simple truths—love, faith, hope, gratitude, truthfulness, kindness, forgiveness, peace, and prayer—since these were the way to happiness.

Papa's house had several rooms but one was his alone, a place where he went to meditate and commune with spirit. Papa and Joseph usually sat in the front room as grandfather taught him lessons, but one day Grandfather surprised Joseph when he opened the door to his private sanctuary and invited him in.

Joseph entered the room reverently; it felt strange to be there, knowing how very special this room was to Grandfather. Wide-eyed, Joseph looked around. The room was dim. Gradually his eyes adjusted and Joseph intently took in all he saw. He was surprised that the room was stark, strangely empty. The wood floor, buffed to a shine, was bare except for a throw rug, which lay in front of a large leather chair.

The big chair faced a wall. On that wall hung a painting of Christ, rich in glorious colors. Beneath the picture sat a small table. The table's warm patina complemented the ornate carvings on its legs. From across the room Joseph couldn't tell whether they were figures of flowers and leaves or if they were angels with long flowing hair. Joseph wondered if perhaps Papa had brought the painting and the table with him from Italy.

Papa told Joseph to sit on the floor, instructing him to watch. When Joseph began to ask why, Papa put his finger to his lips, shushing him to silence. Grandfather then walked to the oversized leather chair and sat down. Joseph watched as his grandfather began to perform a ritual that he had never before seen.

Papa raised both hands above his head and began to rub his forehead. As he did, he began breathing, slowly and deeply. After a few minutes, he dropped his hands, one to the chair's armrest, and the other to his chest. Papa made the sign of the cross and voiced a prayer, which he repeated several times. With his stare fixed on the table, grandfather's gaze grew more and more intense—so intense Joseph could no longer recognize his grandfather's eyes. The familiar eyes that always held tenderness for him had now become those of a stranger.

Time passed slowly and Joseph began to get restless. Grandfather was taking what seemed to be forever. Then, just when it looked as if he was falling asleep with his eyes wide open, Grandfather suddenly put one hand out in front of him. He pointed, motioning for Joseph to look. Next, he pointed to the table, crooked his finger back and forth, bending and straightening it several times, as if he were ordering the little table to come forward.

Joseph rubbed his eyes. He could hardly believe what he saw. The table began to move! It was as if it understood what Grandfather had wanted. Slowly but steadily the little table glided across the smooth wooden floor.

Joseph thought his eyes were playing tricks on him. He closed them tight and rubbed them again, briskly this time. Opening his eyes and blinking, he saw that the table was still moving. It kept coming forward until Grandfather put up his hand and willed it to stop!

Joseph's mouth dropped open—it was so dry he couldn't speak. When finally he got his voice back, he ran to his grandfather. Excited, he repeatedly asked him, "How did you do that, Papa? Will you teach me to do it? Will you, Papa, will you?"

Papa smiled and Joseph saw his grandfather's eyes soften back into the old familiar ones he knew. Grandfather laughed heartily, ruffled Joseph's hair and hugged him tenderly, but did not give him an answer.

Although he did not understand how his grandfather had managed to move the table without touching it, this incident left an unforgettable image in his mind. So memorable was the demonstration that later in life when Joseph opened an office for psychic research, he was eager to explore ways to develop and use the powers of his own mind.

As Joseph grew older, Papa taught him to use his mind to communicate with spirit. He told him of spirit guides and of the seven planes of existence. He explained that with the exception of Earth, the physical plane, the planes were spiritual and occupied by souls at various levels of development. Found in the higher planes, he stated, were spirit guides, such as those that would eventually accompany and help Joseph.

Papa described the planes of existence as follows:

1. Physical plane: Earth, where we come to experience life's lessons. More than a few lifetimes will be spent on this plane until a soul realizes that material possessions matter little.

2. Astral plane: where most spirits remain after passing from this world. Here the soul learns control over the lower emotions of hate, jealousy, and greed.

3. Causal plane: where thoughts, desires, and emotions are purified.

4. Mental plane: where the soul learns the purpose of its existence.

5. Intuitional plane: where the soul loses interest in material things and begins its spiritual journey.

6. Spiritual plane: an advanced plane where the soul finds love, understanding, truth, and wisdom.

7. Divine plane: the highest plane—the realm the soul seeks. Here one finds those that radiate light—God, angels, and spirits of rarefied form.

Papa told Joseph that future events he would see will have already taken place in the ether. He explained, "It is in the ether that spirit works; things take place in the ether before they manifest here on earth. All space throughout the universe—space that our eyes perceive as empty—is full, filled with ether." [This aspect of Papa's mystical understanding of space has since been corroborated by science. Scientists at NASA believe that invisible dark energy and dark matter (what Papa called "ether") make up 95 percent of the universe—68 percent is dark energy, 27 percent is dark matter—and the remaining 5 percent is composed of matter that can be observed. Further, dark energy, although invisible, has weight and is never lost or destroyed.]

Papa explained to Joseph that knowledge of the planes of existence was secretly passed down by heads of churches and leaders of clandestine societies who also knew of other principles, such as the Law of Attraction. This law describes how energy reacts to the thoughts on which we focus, bringing us more of the same. "The thoughts we hold in our minds become our beliefs because we have accepted them." Papa asserted, adding, "As written in Proverbs 23:7: 'For as he [man] thinketh within himself, so is he.'"[1]

Papa believed that those who held political or religious power refused to divulge this secret openly. By keeping it hidden, they managed to maintain the status quo, ensuring the elite their wealth and the dominance of their professions, thus keeping the masses under control, working at physically demanding jobs and ignorant of how the power of thought could transform their lives. He said that those 'in the know' "jealously guarded the secret and were quick to label diviners as witches or evildoers, preferring to kill them rather than allow them power or to divulge the secret."

Papa offered too that "when God created the universe he formed a network, and within this network was the ether. He said the ether provides the conduit between the physical and the mental planes so that soul, mind, thought, spirit, consciousness, stars, planets, suns, moons—all are connected."

Papa may have been right when he said all things are connected. In his book *How the Hippies Saved Physics*, David Kaiser writes of discoveries quantum scientists have made while experimenting with subatomic particles. Findings show that when a photon is split into two halves and one of the halves is exposed to a stimulus, the other half reacts instantaneously and in the same manner, no matter how great the distance is between the two.[2]

Papa told Joseph that since the dawn of the Christian era, people in power had hidden the truth about reincarnation. Centuries ago men of religion hid this truth in order to make humankind believe they had been given but one lifetime in which to spiritually advance, one chance in which to work out their problems before facing Judgment Day. Fear of this day kept the populace submissive. Joseph believed it would take many lifetimes to learn all of life's lessons. He believed that we keep coming back until we learn how to get along with each other.

As a young boy, Joseph listened to his grandfather. However, it was not until later in life that Joseph discovered how precious these lessons were. It was also later that he realized it was Grandfather's faith that had gotten the family through the hard times.

HARD TIMES

W ord of Papa Plaia's amazing powers and his ability to perform healings
had followed him from Sicily to Chicago. Soon neighbors were stopping
by to ask him for advice, guidance, and occasionally a healing. Few of them had
money, so instead they paid Papa with food or a job bartered for his service.

Life was hard during the Depression, and money was scarce. Often Joseph
pulled a wagon through the alleys in search of glass and scrap metal to salvage
for pocket change. Although the family had little, Papa would not allow negative
thoughts in his household. He would admonish any negativity by ordering family
members to "push those thoughts out of your mind—don't let them take hold."

Papa's conviction was contagious. It seemed to Joseph that the sheer power of
his faith pushed negativity away. Papa reminded the family daily to count their
blessings, advising them not to be discouraged, that God would get them through
the bad times. Survive they did, but hard times persisted.

One night when Caterina's youngest son, Tony, was five years old, she awoke
from a terrifying dream in which she saw he had been hit by a truck. Shaken by
the dream, she warned Joseph and Nick—now eight and twelve years old—that
if the boys went outside something bad was sure to happen, and she made them
promise to remain indoors that day. Yet, as soon as she left for work, Nick and
Joseph ran out of the house, taking their brother Tony with them.

Nick and Joseph ran down the street with Tony following as fast as his little
legs would go. Occasionally the older boys stopped to make certain their brother
was keeping up, but at one point they crossed a street and turned back just in time
to see Tony jump off the curb straight into the path of an oncoming truck. Brakes
squealed, and Tony screamed as the truck hit him, badly crushing one of his legs.
The boys ran back scared out of their wits, remembering the warning their mother
had given them.

At work, Joseph's mother felt the accident when it happened. She ran to the supervisor's office, saying she had to leave because her baby boy had been hurt. The supervisor didn't know what to think. He'd heard many excuses to get out of work but never one like this.

He ordered Caterina to return to her work. She insisted he listen to her. Then the phone rang. When the supervisor heard a voice asking to speak with "Mrs. DeLouise," he was dumbstruck. The man on the phone said a truck had hit her son. Caterina screamed, "My son, my baby—please let me go!"

When she arrived at the scene of the accident, she discovered an ambulance had already taken Tony to the hospital. Caterina had been fighting back tears, but when she saw the same truck and police officer she had seen in her dream, she began to sob. Just as the officer began to explain to her what had happened, she spotted Nick and Joseph peeking around a corner, already frightened and distraught at seeing their mother so upset. Caterina ordered them to go home and wait for her.

Little Tony's leg was so badly shattered the doctors had to insert a piece of metal into it so it would grow back properly. The memory of bringing pain to his brother and mother forever remained with Joseph.

When he was ten, Joseph had another terrifying experience. On that fateful day, Joseph was waiting for two of his close friends to stop by. The three of them had plans to go to Goose Island, a place near their home where sand was stored in piles beneath elevated train tracks. None of their parents knew they played there. In fact, it was so secluded no one knew they were there, making it the perfect place for their "kingdom." Each time a train car dumped its contents, huge mounds of sand formed below. As a train pulled in, the boys would scurry up the mound and delight in having the new load of sand come rushing over their legs. They laughed at the train, dubbing themselves "kings."

Joseph loved going to Goose Island, especially on hot days when the tracks shaded the sun and cooled their kingdom below. However, on that day he looked out the screen door and said to his friends, "Don't go to Goose Island today, guys. It's not safe. Something bad is going to happen. Stay here and we'll find something else to do."

His friends stared at him in disbelief. "Bad?" they asked, laughing. "Joseph's afraid of *something bad!*" they mocked. They knew Joseph loved playing there as much as they did.

After all, they were "kings," and kings weren't afraid of anything. Unable to figure out what was wrong, they looked at each other the way boys do when they want to show they're not afraid of anything, and then began laughing and poking fun. Amidst their banter, one of them shouted, "Whadja do to get grounded, Joe?

Didja come home late again?" "We'll see you tomorrow!" yelled the other boy as they rushed off, hooting and hollering.

They turned back once and shouted, "Sissy!" and then were gone before Joseph could convince them of the feeling he had inside—that it was not safe for them to go there that day.

When his mother came home from work, she sensed something was wrong with Joseph. When she asked him about it, Joseph replied that he was just tired, so Caterina went about making dinner. That evening, Joseph was sitting on the porch with Papa when he saw the parents of his friends approaching the house. Knowing that they were looking for their boys, he ran to his room saying his stomach hurt. He knew what was wrong and began to cry. Between his sobs, Joseph's mother coaxed the story from her son. He told her how he had tried to tell his friends not to go to Goose Island; that a bad thing was going to happen. He explained that paying attention to the feeling of danger that had swept over him had saved his life, and he wished he could have convinced his friends to listen to him.

When Caterina told this to the boys' parents, they asked Joseph and his father to come with them to Goose Island to help look for their sons. Upon arriving, they called out and searched the area, but there was no sign of the boys. Finally it grew dark and the parents decided to return home, hoping their sons were horsing around somewhere closer to home.

The next day, when the boys failed to appear, their parents called the police. Joseph went with them to Goose Island to show the police where they played, explaining they jumped around on the piles of sand until a train pulled in, then stood beneath it and let the sand pour down and cover their legs.

As they approached the piles of sand, a strange feeling came over Joseph, pulling him to a spot where he and his friends had never played. Joseph pointed to the area and told the police, "They're there."

It turned out that his friends had played where no sand had built up to deflect a train's load—no mound to distribute the weight or disperse the grains of fresh sand. Rather than spreading gently over their legs, the load of sand plummeted straight down on top of the boys, quickly burying them. As the police uncovered their bodies, Joseph felt as if his friends were still there. He swore he could hear them laughing and calling each other "kings."

Joseph's heart ached over the passing of his friends, yet he knew they were still alive in spirit. Even at that young age, Joseph seemed to know that death was not the end.

TEEN YEARS

As the Depression wore on, everyone in Joseph's household did what they could to earn money and keep the family together. Caterina worked in a factory. Mike worked whenever and wherever he could. Nick brought in money as well. And Joseph, by age twelve, was selling newspapers and neckties on the streets and delivering groceries in the neighborhood.

Night after night on his way home from work, Joseph passed a small shop with two beautiful lamps in the window. He dreamed of buying them for his mother, and one day his dream came true. After purchasing a necktie, a man unexpectedly gave Joseph a generous tip, telling him to keep the change. Adding the tip to his savings, Joseph finally had the money he needed for the lamps. He shoved the fortune into his pocket and ran to the shop to buy the treasures.

Racing home with his gift, all he could think of was his mother's happiness upon seeing the beautiful lamps. Joseph rushed in and gave her his gift, eager for her to laugh and dance in circles as she had when he'd found the buried treasure. Instead, his mother held him close and began to cry. Joseph was confused. He didn't understand that she was happy for the gift but sad because their family desperately needed that money for more practical items.

Soon after he turned thirteen, local gangs allowed Joseph to join in their favorite pastime—shooting dice. While most of the boys in Joseph's neighborhood traveled in gangs, Joseph knew his mother wouldn't approve of his associating with them, so he made sure to roll dice in alleys far from home. He did not want to ever again risk disappointing his mother.

The gangs were tough, some more so than others. The tougher gangs either had close brushes with the police and been placed on the police watch list, or had begun making a name for themselves with members of the mob. They laughed and bragged about how stupid the cops were and how many times they escaped being caught. While Joseph wasn't a member of a gang, he found it exciting just to know them.

In the alleys, Joseph loved the feel of the dice in his hand and the thrill of tossing them. As it turned out, he was good at the game. Whenever he had saved enough spare change, Joseph would head out to play. One evening in particular turned out to be especially lucrative. As he played, he felt strange—like his feet weren't touching the ground. It was as if he were floating, watching the game from above. Time after time he tossed the dice and won. He could see which numbers would come up before they left his hand. He didn't understand what was happening.

That night Joseph won all the money, cleaning everyone out. When the game broke up, Joseph and his friends headed home. As soon as they were out of earshot of the others, his friends excitedly questioned him, wanting to know "What happened back there, Joe?" "What got into you?" "You scared the hell out of us." One of the boys exclaimed, "What was going on with your eyes, Joe? They looked strange, as if they didn't belong to you. You looked like you were possessed!"

Joseph couldn't explain it to himself, let alone to his friends. He only knew he felt weird, lightheaded. It was as if an entity had controlled his hand. He knew beforehand that he was going to win; he sensed that he couldn't lose.

After that experience, Joseph didn't return to the alleys. He knew the gangs would never again let him "walk" with their money. He was done with gambling.

As Joseph matured and became more responsible, he remained close with several friends but steered clear of the gangs. He avoided trouble, mostly out of respect for his mother. More and more he realized that from the time he was born his mother thought of him as special. He couldn't bear the thought of making her unhappy—it would break her heart.

Joseph had inherited his grandfather's charisma and his good looks as well—clear blue eyes, a striking Roman nose, and a big, broad, beautiful smile. A neatly trimmed beard covered his chin, complimented by the small V-shaped tuft of hair he groomed beneath his lower lip. A thick head of dark wavy hair topped off his slim body, adding the final addition to his good looks. Taking after his grandfather in character as well, Joseph grew into a compassionate and highly ethical youth. His upbringing had molded him into a young man of principle; his personality, a product of his environment of love and faith.

However, as much as he loved his family, Joseph was in a hurry to experience life. So, as soon as he turned seventeen, he joined the Navy to see the world.

An Unexpected Battle

⸻

Joseph served his Navy duty in the Pacific on the USS *Taussig, DD-746,* a destroyer—or "tin can" in navy slang. While stationed at Guam Naval Base, it was once again a premonition that saved his life.

Assigned the duty of unloading ammunition from the ship's bunker, Joseph and two of his friends worked below deck, handing it topside to others, who in turn handed it off for transport to storage. Like pails of water on a fire line, the ammo traveled from sailor to sailor until it eventually reached its destination.

One morning, Joseph awoke in a sweat as a feeling of danger swept over him. Heeding the feeling, Joseph decided not to go to work that day and warned his friends something was wrong. He told them of the forewarning he'd received, recounting the story of Goose Island and comparing the feeling he had now with the one he had then. He desperately tried to convince his friends not to report for work that day.

Looking at him with suspicion, his friends warned him to stop talking about "that stuff." "Tell us the truth," one of them demanded. "Just admit you're feeling lazy today." Chiming in, his other friend said, "I wouldn't want to be in your shoes when you try to sell this one. Wise up. Come to work with us." Refusing to listen, they headed off to the bunker.

Joseph reported to sickbay and imparted his feeling to a suspicious medical officer, who responded that he wasn't about to buy into a cockamamie story like that and ordered him back to work. Midway into his reprimand, however, an explosion rocked the air from below deck. Running to the scene, Joseph found the below deck blast had killed both of his buddies and seriously injured several other sailors' topside. Once again, Joseph suffered the devastation of not being able to save his friends.

In 1947, Joseph's Navy duty ended and he hurried back to Chicago with the dream of starting a business. He had plans to work and save money until he had enough to strike out on his own. It didn't matter to him what kind of business it was; Joseph was certain whatever he did he would be able to make a go of it.

However, Joseph had returned home from the service with a cough that soon became more serious. The doctor's diagnosis: advanced-stage tuberculosis. Now facing a new and unexpected battle, Joseph spent nearly two years in a sanitarium enduring well-intended but uncomfortable medical treatments. The daily routine began with a round of forced coughing, with his head and chest lowered in an effort to bring up sputum that had settled in his lungs during the night. The next procedure involved covering his chest with bags of sand to limit expansion of his lungs in an effort to contain the spread of the tuberculosis. In those days there was no cure for the illness other than fresh air, rest, palliative treatment, and prayer. Joseph felt certain the tuberculosis would have killed him were it not for two miracles.

The first was the miracle of love. While confined in the sanitarium, he fell madly in love with a young, beautiful girl who worked there. Caterina wasn't happy with the romance, but since this girl seemed to give her son the will to live, she held her tongue and said nothing. Many long and arduous months passed. Caterina spent every possible hour by her son's side trying to bring him comfort. She prayed constantly, keeping close watch while Joseph clung to life.

Then the second miracle took place. Late one night while Joseph slept, a Chinese doctor came into his room. He walked past Caterina, going straight to Joseph's bedside. The doctor checked Joseph's vital signs, listened to his lungs, and then spent quite some time standing over him, silently watching as he breathed. Next, the doctor turned to speak with Caterina. He told the worried and exhausted mother that her son would soon get better.

The next day, Joseph's mother excitedly told the attending house doctor about the visit from the Chinese doctor. The doctor looked at Caterina strangely, feeling stress and lack of sleep may have seriously altered her perceptions. He told her that there was no Chinese doctor working at the sanitarium and insisted that Caterina immediately go home and rest.

One week later, a new antibiotic drug became available for use. Streptomycin proved to be a miracle drug for tuberculosis patients, including Joseph. After treatment with streptomycin, Joseph slowly began to recover. A few weeks later, the doctors announced they were certain he would regain his full health. Within months Joseph was healed.

Joseph and the girl of his dreams wed on December 26, 1948, there in the sanitarium. The marriage lasted less than two months, however, because his new wife, who fancied herself in show business, left to pursue her dream. The divorce caused Joseph to break from the Roman Catholic Church into which he was born. [Annulment is the only recourse allowed by the church for divorcing Catholics who want to remarry. Once divorced, Catholics can remarry in a civil ceremony, but to do so goes against Catholic doctrine and they forfeit their rights as Catholics. Joseph disagreed with this, separating himself forever from the church.]

In 1949 Joseph decided to use the GI Bill to attend beauty school and become a hairdresser. While at the school, Joseph met Helen, who would become his second wife. Helen was one of those models hired for the students to practice their hairdressing skills on. Joseph immediately picked her as *his* model.

His first few attempts at working on Helen's hair were less than successful—the permanent was frizzy, the haircut wasn't much better, and when he first dyed Helen's hair, she ended up with a head full of different colored streaks.

Luckily, Helen was a good sport. Despite the hair disasters, Joseph persisted—not only in styling her hair but in wooing her. Within a year, he and Helen were married.

WILLIE

Upon graduating from beauty school, Joseph worked at Steven's Powder Box, a downtown Chicago beauty shop located in the Stevens Building, at 17 North State Street. There he met fellow hairdresser Willie. The two quickly became best friends.

Wilhelm "Willie" Gehrig, a quiet man born in Germany, hated war and had come to America to find peace. As a young man in Germany during World War I, he was drafted into the army and forced into battle. After marching to the front, his troop came under brutal attack, leaving nearly all of the men either dead or dying. Willie survived but suffered severely from the horrors he had experienced. Upon returning home, he resolved never again to fight or harm another human being. Willie sought out a famed female mystic and embarked on a spiritual journey. Studying under her guidance for nearly two years, Willie perfected his psychic abilities in meditation, healing, and methods of channeling spirit.

When the mystic felt her death was imminent, she bequeathed Willie her two most prized crystals—one miniature, the other large. The larger crystal was superb; despite its size, it was perfectly clear with no imperfections. The smaller one, with multiple light-reflecting facets, could easily slip inside a pocket.

Shortly after his tutor's death, Willie moved to the United States, where he met and married the love of his life, a kind and lovely woman who had also emigrated from Germany. Sadly, after only a few years of marriage, death took Willie's beloved wife. Devastated, Willie vowed never to remarry; indeed, he never did.

While meditating, Willie communicated often with his deceased wife, content in knowing she was with him. At such times, Willie wrote beautiful poems she dictated to him, some of them in English, although most were written in his native German. Over the years, the stack of poems grew, nearly filling a box eight inches deep.

Willie was a sensitive person. He and Joseph got along well. In addition to styling his clients' hair at the Powder Box, Willie also gave healings and spiritual readings to those he'd known for a long time. Joseph, for his part, soon discovered that as he worked with his clients' hair, he was receiving psychic vibrations. Curious, he asked his clients if they'd let him "guess" things about themselves and people in their lives. The women loved the idea, so Joseph began to tell them things such as the number of children they had, whether they were boys or girls, when they would be taking a trip, and where they would go. Joseph soon began to attract attention not only for his hairstyling but also for his psychic abilities. Word spread, and his clientele grew quickly.

Joseph and Willie worked together for nearly a year. At the end of 1951, they decided to open their own beauty shop, calling it Mr. Joseph's Styling Salon. "Mr. Joseph" was a nickname Joseph's clients had given him. Loyal customers followed them to the new shop, which flourished. Business was good, and Joseph had no difficulty supporting his growing family.

Willie had long before taken a special interest in Joseph's psychic abilities. Joseph highly regarded Willie and looked upon him not only as a friend but also as a spiritual mentor. Two nights a week after closing the shop, they stayed to talk. Willie shared the knowledge he had learned years before from his tutor in Germany, teaching Joseph how to conduct séances, use crystal balls, and channel spirit.

Before long, two nights a week turned into three. By then, Willie and Joseph were regularly conducting séances for their clients and attending meetings at the Fellowship of Spiritual Frontiers. Many evenings Joseph spent alone, a habit carried over from childhood. Although Joseph dearly loved his wife and children, he also had a penchant for solitude.

Gradually, after eighteen years, Joseph and Helen's marriage began to unravel. They now had six children, one boy and five girls. By this time Joseph had made public four tragic predictions: the collapse of the Silver Bridge, the Manteno train crash, the drowning at Chappaquiddick, and the midair collision of two planes. Each prediction had brought with it ridicule as well as notoriety.

Perhaps Helen could no longer bear the neighbors' taunts or the harassment of her children. Maybe she had grown weary of being shunned—or of being left alone. Joseph had been spending more and more time away from the family.

Whatever the reason, their marriage ended in divorce.

A Visit from Spirit

D ivorce hit Joseph hard, bringing back memories of his first failed marriage. Earlier in his life he had been able to turn to his grandfather for advice. Now that Papa had passed, Joseph turned to his mother. She advised him to seek guidance in prayer, so over the next few weeks Joseph set aside a part of each day to pray.

One evening while on his knees intently praying for direction, three spirits suddenly appeared, hovering side-by-side in the air slightly above Joseph. Hooded robes partially draped their faces. However, Joseph didn't need to see their features to know who they were. Psychically he knew they were Saint Joseph in the middle, Saint Francis to his right, and Padre Pio to his left.

Their presence, charging the atmosphere with love, hope, and encouragement, had a calming effect on Joseph. He felt they were friends he could trust and to whom he could bare his soul. He poured out his doubts and his worries to them, imparting how he felt he had failed in his marriage. He wondered what God would want with him now that he had failed in life.

The spirits assured him all was well and that this was the time for him to give up his hair salon, increase his psychic work, and develop direct voice mediumship.

Joseph said he wanted to serve God, but questioned the spirits about his capacity to make a living at psychic work. The thought of giving up his hair salon frightened Joseph; it had grown into a prosperous business, and he needed money to take care of his children. His responsibilities weighed heavily on his mind.

The spirits answered him in the form of a question. "Have we ever let you down, Joseph? Haven't we always taken care of you?"

Joseph shamefully hung his head and whispered, "Yes."

The spirits immediately replied, "Yes, we have, and we always will. We will always be there for you."

Joseph humbly asked, "Am I worthy to guide others? Will I have the answers they need?" The three replied, "Spirit will provide the answers."

They advised Joseph to move forward with his life and not look back. The past was past. He was to continue the work he was born to do in this lifetime.

With that, the three vanished as quickly as they had appeared. There was no time to ask more questions, nor was there any need to ask. The spirits had spoken, confirming that Joseph was destined to fulfill the spiritual missions he had learned in his childhood. Shaken, Joseph silently vowed to do as the spirits said.

When Joseph told Willie about the visit, he was still torn. He was happy at the beauty shop—he loved the clientele, the joking, the camaraderie, and he needed the money—yet he also felt a spiritual tug. Willie knew the time had come for his friend to follow his destiny and that he would soon shed his misgivings. He handed Joseph his two cherished crystals, insisting he take them as a gift. Willie's vote of confidence finally convinced Joseph that indeed he must follow his calling.

Joseph's predictions continued, and the press took more and more notice. As his fame escalated along with acknowledgment for his work, his reluctance to talk about forthcoming tragedies ended. No longer was he hesitant to speak of his predictions. In fact, he now looked forward to talking with reporters—perhaps a little too eagerly. Joseph was caught up in the swell of excitement and loved every minute of it.

Then one night the three spirits visited again, this time in a dream. In the dream, the three spirits stood in front of and slightly above Joseph. Looking down at him, they said nothing. Indeed, no words were needed. Their silence was the message, and it had a profound effect on Joseph. He took it as a warning. Seeking fame would put him at risk of blocking his psychic connection with the spirit world.

The dream startled Joseph awake. Humbly recalling that this might be God's way of drawing attention to the unknown, Joseph set aside his vanity and vowed to redouble his efforts in guiding people to the spiritual side of life.

Never again would he let his ego get in the way of practicing his psychic work.

MIND UNLIMITED

In the early 1970s, Joseph opened an office all on his own, dedicating it to psychic research and development. He named it 'Mind Unlimited' in honor of his grandfather who had taught him about the power of the mind. Initially Joseph worked there only in the evenings, taking appointments at his beauty shop during the day to balance and ground himself, and to help him meet his financial obligations until feeling comfortable in moving into full-time psychic work.

When he opened his psychic practice, three crystal balls adorned his office—the two that Willie had given him and one that belonged to Papa, which was given a place of prominence on Joseph's desk. The crystal reminded Joseph of Papa's advice that people had free will and needed to make their own choices. Joseph's role was to guide people to their own truths, to help them discover that they themselves had the answers to their questions. When clients asked if a spouse or a lover was cheating, Joseph felt it was not his place to reply. Choosing to focus on the positive, he would instead suggest ways in which his clients might mend their situations, offering to work with them toward achieving that goal.

Joseph kept his messages simple. He did not use big words to sound important. Rather, he spoke caringly to people in language that came from the heart as he guided them toward their passion and purpose in life.

He also kept the pledge that his mother had made to St. Joseph when she promised her son would live a life of service to him. To clients who expressed interest, he would give a miniature statue of the saint, along with a copy of the *Prayers to St. Joseph*, which was found in AD 50 and sent in 1505 AD from the pope to Emperor Charles while going into battle:

"Oh, St. Joseph, whose protection is so great, so strong, so prompt
before the throne of God, I place in thee all my interests and desires.

"Oh, St. Joseph, assist me by thy powerful intercession and obtain for me all spiritual blessings through thy foster Son, Jesus Christ, our Lord, so that, having engaged here below thy heavenly power, I may offer thee my thanksgiving and homage.

"Oh, St. Joseph, I never weary contemplating thee and Jesus asleep in thine arms. I dare not approach while He reposes near thy heart. Press Him in my name and kiss His fine head for me, and ask Him to return the kiss when I draw my dying breath. St. Joseph, Patron of departing souls—pray for me. Amen"[3]

As soon as Joseph opened the door to his new psychic office, he was busy. A long list of beauty shop clients came to him for psychic readings, along with a host of new clients. And Willie, who had a keen interest in seeing Joseph carry on the work, visited often.

As time went on, Joseph found the perfect centerpiece for his office—beautiful three-foot statues of St. Joseph and St. Mary splendidly painted in glorious colors. The statues, surrounded by lighted candles, were displayed on a table against the far wall, directly ahead as one entered the office, making them the first thing people saw.

When clients came to see Joseph at his Mind Unlimited office, he gave them his psychic impression as honestly and positively as possible. If the future he saw didn't look good, he'd find a way to tell them gently, giving them hope along with a plan to begin working on their problem.

Joseph found hope in every situation. He would redirect a worried person's attention to small changes they could make on their own until they became strong enough to resolve the problem. Although the answers were obvious to Joseph, he felt it far better to offer others guidance that helped them solve their problems themselves. The one exception to this practice was if he saw danger or harm coming to a client or their loved ones. In that case, he would step in and let the person know what to do for protection.

People were comfortable with Joseph. They found solace in talking with him. Many looked upon him as a confessor to whom they could safely express guilty feelings. He spent the better part of one morning talking a determined and desperate man out of committing a crime for money, a crime he had planned to carry out that very night. Joseph was able to turn the man around and show him a better way. As well, a client who was contemplating suicide gave up that thought after talking with Joseph. Clinging to the hope he found in Joseph's words, he became a regular visitor to Joseph's office. Those who had been born the wrong gender found acceptance and understanding in Joseph when others were quick to condemn them.

Often clients sought Joseph's help in finding a soul mate. When they told Joseph they were looking for love, he would stop them and ask, "How about looking for 'like'?" He'd continue, saying that "like" comes before "love," advising that they first look to be "in like" with a person. He cautioned them about infatuation, saying, "Oftentimes infatuation is misconstrued for love; we skip the feeling of 'like' and immediately jump to thoughts of love. It can be hard to tell the difference between true love and the first blush—the fascination we feel when caught up in a rush of attraction—a chemical reaction that comes on quickly and can wane just as fast." When clients would say their horoscope predicted that love was "just around the corner," Joseph would caution, "Horoscopes are fine, but it will take more than that to find a soul mate."

He taught how the Law of Attraction works, explaining, "You can't just send your thoughts out to the ether then sit back and wait for things to happen. While it is true that spirit will work on your thoughts and the universe will help guide that person to you, you must also take an active role in the process. The Law of Attraction goes beyond positive thinking and wishing. It requires that you picture that which you desire as having already manifested.

"Envision this frequently until your subconscious mind believes it is true. Feel the happiness of knowing that your wish has become a reality. Repeat this daily—several times a day if time allows—until both your conscious and your unconscious mind accept it as true."

He would then advise his clients not to falter in their thoughts—not to put limitations on desires or try to bargain with the universe by saying, "I want this, but only if it means…" or "I desire this, but not if…."

He would insist: "You must be clear from the beginning about exactly what it is you are wishing for before putting it out into the ether, and then hold fast to your wish. The universe is powerful and brings us the things on which we focus our thoughts, whether positive or negative. Keep a close check on your thoughts and be sure to keep them positive."

He encouraged people to open themselves to the world, to join the mainstream of life, to get out and meet new people. He often advised women to "take a class, join a group, volunteer; attend an antique auction or a car show"—whatever interested them. "If they were not actively searching," he said, "they would not find their soul mate." "Finding a soul mate is not an instantaneous occurrence," he would caution. "It takes effort and may take a little time."

Joseph wanted people to follow their hearts, but to take it slowly and give love the test of time. He advised his clients to "allow love to prove itself," counseling, "Get to know the other person before becoming seriously involved. Go out together on dates, have fun, and take your time getting to know one another."

When asked how to recognize a soul mate, Joseph would tell them, "True soul mates accept each other, loving one another exactly as they are. A true soul mate wants the best for the other person and encourages them to grow." He would then add, "We build relationships over a period of time. Finding true love takes patience; lasting feelings take time to develop."

Joseph said, "The soul recognizes its true soul mate from the vibrations our heart sends to our soul. The soul changes the heart's vibrations into a feeling like the feeling we get when we meet someone new and know right away that we like them as a person. The feeling is similar to this, but deeper and much more intense." He said, "This knowledge comes from deep within. Learn to trust your inner feelings."

He believed that true soul mates had been together many times, both in the physical and in the astral worlds, helping each other with their spiritual growth. "It's as if you have always known one another—that you have been together before and, now that you've found each other again, you feel complete."

Finally, he told his clients that not all the soul mates who come into their lives would be with them for romance—that soul mates sometimes come as friends, helpers, teachers, or even challengers, providing an opportunity for soul growth. "There are times when a soul mate will enter a life for just a short period of time." He added, "It's not always meant to be permanent."

Most of the clients who came to Joseph's office sought psychic readings. When he gave a reading, Joseph would hold the person's hand or ask to hold an object they owned, such as a watch or a ring. This allowed Joseph to psychically perceive the vibrations of the person, giving him an awareness of the conditions and emotions surrounding them. Joseph said the first impression was most important, as it was the strongest and opened the way to more.

His readings lasted about an hour. During that time, Joseph would tell the person of the things he saw and give them advice on how best to handle their situation, guiding them in a direction that would end in positive results. At times Joseph would receive a picture that would tell the story.

A woman once asked if her new boyfriend would marry her. The image Joseph received was of a man and woman bound together with a ribbon tied to their wrists, a sure sign of a joining.

Another woman asked if a particular person who had befriended her at work could be trusted. No sooner did Joseph close his eyes than he came back with the answer. The picture he had received was of barbed wire twisted into a bundle, indicating this person was not trustworthy.

Not every picture he received presented a clear interpretation. Joseph told me he had learned to rely on his intuition for answers; he said if he began to intellectualize the things he saw, the flow of information became blocked. He had learned not to question but rather to go with his feelings.

At times clients became upset because something Joseph told them during their reading had not yet materialized—weeks or even months had passed—and they were convinced it never would. For example, one client asked Joseph for his advice regarding her husband's business. It had been going downhill for quite a while, and the woman was worried it would be their financial ruin. Joseph told her not to worry, that he saw her living in a warm climate in a big comfortable home with plenty of money. Five months after her reading, the woman demanded her money back, saying her husband had lost his business and they were now bankrupt. She went on to say she felt Joseph had taken her money and "told her a story" just to make her feel better. Joseph returned her money and did not expect to hear from her again.

Less than two years later, however, the woman called back and sheepishly apologized, saying Joseph had been right. Her husband had passed away soon after the bankruptcy. Penniless, she was forced to go and live with her daughter in Florida, where she eventually married a wealthy retired widower. She told Joseph she was now living in a beautiful home and had no worries about money or her future.

At the time Joseph provided this woman with this reading, he had not seen her husband with her in her new home. He didn't mention this since he knew she was unhappy about the state of their failing business, and the thought crossed his mind that she might be considering divorce. Not wanting to influence her decision or empower negative thoughts, his mind worked to find the positive impression he had relayed to her.

Clients often contacted Joseph years afterward to tell him that what he predicted had finally materialized, though not within the time frame they had expected.

Following one such incident, Joseph told me that in other realms, time does not work as it does in our world, and it is therefore difficult for a psychic to pinpoint precisely when an event will occur. He said that time on earth differs significantly from time in the spirit realm. During one of his out-of-body astral travels, Joseph penetrated a dimension where the past, present, and future exist together. There he observed the passage of time, astonished that he was not moving through time but rather that time was passing through him. He described it as standing on the corner of a street waiting to cross, and, without moving, suddenly finding yourself on the other side, amazed that the street has passed through you. Even more fascinating, he found he could stop time, start it again, move it faster, or slow it down—all at his command.

Most clients who came to see Joseph were women. Joseph was a longtime advocate of women, whom he felt didn't have the same advantages as men, so he steered many into professions that were more rewarding and offered higher pay. For example, he guided them toward careers in banking, real estate, and the stock market, which were male-dominated professions in those days.

To women who desired a fuller life, he advised they get out of the house, take a part-time job, or get involved with their community or church. He frequently counseled women to volunteer their time at a hospital or work for a charity. Others he counseled to go back to school and further their education.

Pointing women toward opportunities for happiness, more often than not he saw that excitement—sometimes even romance—would accompany their new endeavors.

One day a strong, confident, and independent woman named Sonja walked into Joseph's office. Sonja had already begun making her way in the world and had come to Joseph for help publishing a book of poems she had written. It turned out that Sonja also had a keen interest in psychic phenomena. She had recently returned from a trip to the Philippines, where she had taken her mother to receive a healing from Tony Agpaoa, a famed psychic surgeon who routinely used his hands and psychic powers to make an incision and remove tumors or diseased tissue from a person's body, using neither anesthesia nor scalpel. Her mother's treatment was successful.

When Joseph heard of Sonja's trip, he arranged for her to appear on a television program to speak of her mother's experience in the Philippines. Sonja eloquently shared the details of their visit with the viewing audience. She was an instant hit; her personality sparkled. Able to accomplish whatever she set her mind to, she could talk with anyone on any subject and not lose their interest. [Sonja later became Joseph's third wife and the mother of their beloved son Joseph Jr.]

Unlike Sonja, many women who came to Joseph were afraid to step outside the norm. To those he taught: "Never be afraid of making a mistake. Making mistakes is the way we learn and grow. No one in this life is perfect." He often added,

"Remember, we all can learn from another person in this life. Perfect knowledge, on the other hand, is achieved gradually over time, throughout eternity."

Joseph later offered me similar advice about making mistakes. I wanted to apply for a new position at work that had just opened up, but my fear of making a mistake was holding me back. When I voiced my fear during a reading, Joseph looked at me, smiled, and assured me that he wanted me to make mistakes. He said that I would learn from them. His reassurance seemed to take away my fear. I accepted that it wasn't the end of the world to make a mistake. I applied for the job, and I got it. I did make mistakes, but I didn't let them stop me as I would have before. I remembered Joseph's words, did my homework, and soon found myself a respected and valued team member.

PART III
MY JOURNEY

A Life More Common

I grew up in the 1940s in Clifton Park, New York, a small upstate village surrounded by many farms. Our family life was meager. My parents, like many others, struggled to put food on the table. My father was able to find work off and on, but rarely steadily. I remember my mother's excitement when my father once brought home a can of coffee that had fallen off a truck. It had been such a long time since she'd enjoyed a simple cup of coffee.

As a child I was overwhelmingly shy and grew up a loner. Only one other girl my age lived close by. My sister, four years older than me, was not at all happy to have me hanging around her and her friends. Nevertheless, in spite of her protests I tagged along whenever I got the chance. My brother, on the other hand, had several other boys his age to play with.

Back then, things were quite different. Letters were handwritten; telephones were kept on a table or a desk (not slipped into a pocket or a purse); vegetables came fresh from the garden (not from a can on a shelf or a box in the freezer), brown eggs—considered inferior to white eggs—were used only for baking. Television programs were not aired day and night, shows were upbeat and positive, and daily news was not repeatedly broadcast. It was common practice to raise children to be "seen and not heard." There were exceptions, of course, but not in our family. In our home, the children did not join in adult conversation.

I never doubted my mother's love for me. She was a kind and loving parent who found many ways to show me how much she cared. My father, on the other hand, was particularly uncommunicative. So seldom did he address me I can hardly remember an occasion when we spoke.

Because of this, I grew up desperately seeking my father's love and approval. I reasoned that he must love me, since he worked hard to provide for his family and took us fishing on Sundays. However, he never showed feelings of love or caring, which I so craved. Throughout my childhood, I wondered what I had done to make my father treat me in this way, especially when I saw how much my friend's father cared for her. To this day, I still hold the memory of my friend's father picking her up and swinging her high in the air, round and round. I can hear her giggling with joy as her hands clung to the back of her father's neck. My heart ached as I watched them. I longed to have my father pick me up and swing me around or wrap me in his arms and hug me. But this never happened.

Years later my mother told me that my father had grown up in a world where boys were taught that to show love was to show weakness. He hadn't learned to express love and didn't know how to show affection. He'd been raised in a family that used fear—fear of punishment, of the devil, of hell, and of death—to enforce obedience. So fearful was my father at the thought of dying that when he died in his hospital bed in the middle of the night in May 1990, his spirit found its way home to my mother. He appeared before her, telling her he was afraid to go. My mother assured him everything would be all right and that it was safe for him to leave. Before departing, he asked my mother to say the Catholic prayers for him. Soon after she finished her prayers, the phone rang. It was the head nurse at the hospital telling her that her husband had died twenty minutes before. Hearing these things saddened me while at the same time broadened my understanding of the spirit world.

Today, Clifton Park is a pleasant and progressive town, but during my childhood strictness and prejudice permeated the village. Overzealous parents, schoolteachers, ministers, and priests all took turns "keeping an eye"—invariably a critical one. Everyone was your parent. Neighbors watched over each other's children, trying to catch them doing wrong. For a child, the oppression was stifling.

Growing up in this environment did nothing to help me outgrow or overcome my shyness; if anything, it added to it. I was hesitant to speak up or express an opinion. To avoid people, I spent a great deal of time alone, often playing in the woods behind our house. I knew of dark places deep in the woods where trees grew so close together the sun barely shone through. There were places where lilies of the valley carpeted the forest floor, their perfume hanging heavy in the air. I even knew of meadows where endangered lady's slippers flourished.

I knew where to jump the creek without getting my feet wet and how cold the water would be if my foot missed the other bank. Sometimes I'd lie on the grass by the edge of the creek and watch as fat and lazy trout glided slowly downstream. I spent much of my time alone in these woods, communing with nature.

I could identify a bird by its song. I could tell a tree by the shape of its leaf and knew which trees had the best vines for swinging out over deep ravines. I would climb the highest tree without fear. On hot summer afternoons, I'd take a stack of comic books, along with a bag of tomatoes from the garden, and spend the afternoon reading high up in a tree. When I tired of reading, I'd fold leaves into the shape of a box, secure it by the stem, and float ants to the ground.

One day, I discovered a field that no one else seemed to frequent. It was filled with row upon row of mounds covered by long, silky grasses. I thought it belonged to me. Calling it my secret place, I spent much time there.

On one side of the field was a wall built from stones. Vines clung to these stones, their shoots twisting in and out and spreading up and over the wall. There, bunches of large purple grapes, sweeter than any I'd ever tasted, hung in abundance.

I remember running up and down the small hills until I tired and collapsed in the warm grass at the top of a mound. Lying there, I would swish a clutch of cool grapes around my mouth, squeeze the flesh between my teeth, and spit the seeds and skins onto the ground. I can still taste the freshness of the sweet juice as I licked it from my chin.

As heavenly as this sanctuary was for me, getting to the field was not easy. On the way I had to pass a house where two of the ugliest and meanest Scott Terriers lived, so I'd tiptoe past the house as quietly as I could in the hope of not alerting them. On good days they would be inside, and I could slip by unnoticed.

Unfortunately, this was seldom the case. The minute the dogs heard my footsteps they'd come bounding out of the yard, growling and barking with teeth gnashing, one at each of my heels. I'd scramble up the steep bank on the other side of the road, escaping into a thick clump of bushes that grew at the top of the hill.

Luckily I was slender and able to slip in among the bushes. I'd squeeze as close to the center as possible where the dogs' teeth couldn't reach me and stay there for what seemed like hours until they tired of barking. Their energy spent, they'd scamper back to their yard and fall asleep in the sun. I'd delay leaving the safety of the bushes until I felt they were sound asleep, and then I'd venture on.

One sunny day while being held captive by the dogs, I looked down and was amazed to see that the leafy branches of the bushes were covered with large dark blueberries that tasted even sweeter than my grapes. That day, the dogs' barking didn't bother me quite as much.

I spent many happy days in my secret field, scampering up and down each mound, falling to the ground, and resting on the top of one of the little hills. Years later I discovered that the small hills that I so dearly loved were actually the mounded graves of American Indians. When I learned of this, I felt ashamed and guilty for trampling on sacred Indian burial mounds.

I don't know if it was from these Native American mounds or because I spent so much time in solitude, but without realizing it—without even being aware that such a thing was possible—I developed the art of going into a trance. Did my mind commune with the dead Indians as I lay in silence on the mounds? Did I become aware of their spirits while on this sacred ground? Did turning to the silence of my thoughts open me to extrasensory perception? I don't know exactly what provoked my mind to open to psychic awareness.

When I first experienced extrasensory phenomena—things not of the physical world—I was perplexed but not frightened; maybe I was too young to be afraid. Nevertheless, the experiences left me with many questions.

My first otherworldly encounter took place when I was eight years old. One day while playing alone in the backyard of my home, I saw the misty figure of a man suddenly appear in front of me. I thought it must be a ghost, but for some reason I wasn't afraid.

The man wasn't standing on the ground; instead, he hovered above me, about three feet in the air. I could see the upper part of his body and the outline of his legs beneath a long robe; however, the man had no feet. There was nothing but mist where his feet should have been. I thought this strange but was unafraid.

The man smiled at me and then spoke, but his lips were not moving. I heard the words he was saying, but not with my ears. Instead, I heard his words in my mind. Smiling kindly, the man asked, "Do you want to come with me?"

I turned and started to run back toward my friend's house so she could go with me. After going only a few steps, I stopped and asked the man if my friend could come with us. On hearing this, the man smiled again. He looked at me with understanding in his eyes and gently told me, "It's all right. You've forgotten."

With that, he started to disappear. His body disintegrated, breaking into little black dots that slowly faded away. He vanished from the bottom of his robe to the top of his head until he was completely gone.

Although I could no longer see him, the experience left me with a feeling of awe. I didn't tell anyone of my experience until many years later. Upon reading Irish mystic Lorna Byrne's book, *Angels in My Hair*, I came to realize that in my youth I felt much the same as she did. As a child, Byrne could see angels, but she told no one. She felt it was something only she and the angels were meant to share. I also told no one because I felt it was something I alone was supposed to know.

My next otherworldly experience occurred at the age of ten, when I had a near-death experience (NDE), although at the time I didn't know what an NDE was. My sister and I were spending the day with our cousin and her friend. A public swimming pool was close to their home and, since the day was hot, my aunt said it would be all right for us to walk to the pool and swim. I was standing in knee-high water when suddenly something hit me squarely on my back, knocking the breath out of me. I fell forward and landed face down in the pool.

I struggled to surface but couldn't move. I couldn't escape. Whatever had hit me was holding me down under the water. Then I heard my cousin and her friend laughing and giggling and realized that one of them had hit me in the back with both hands and was now sitting on top of me. I fought to get free but couldn't.

I held my breath for as long as possible. My lungs burned for lack of air; it felt as if they were on fire. Fear crowded my mind, and then panic took over. I tried desperately to free myself and get up, but to no avail.

I knew I would have to take a breath soon, but I didn't dare since I was under water! Just as I thought my lungs would burst, a feeling of warmth spread over my body. Peace replaced fear and I grew calm. I remember thinking that everything would be all right. Something inside was telling me, "It's okay, just let go."

I stopped struggling, and everything around me turned to a brilliant rosy pink. Then, suddenly, I was leaving my body and rushing through a tunnel that stretched out far ahead of me. As my body rushed forward, wisps of white floated past me on both sides.

I cannot say how long I was under the water. I don't remember anything after I left my body except for the tunnel. Everything else is a blank. I don't remember being picked up and carried out of the pool, or reentering my body.

When I regained consciousness, I was lying on the concrete deck by the side of the pool with an older man kneeling beside me. One of his arms was beneath my shoulders while the other was turning my body face up. I must have had water in my lungs, since I was coughing and felt dizzy.

As I lay there, the man took my head in one of his hands and looked intently into my eyes. He did not speak. He never said a word the entire time he was with me. The only emotion he showed was a look of concern on his face. He watched me closely until I fully returned to my senses.

As I came around, I coughed and started to sit up, whereupon the man stood up, turned, and slowly walked away into the crowd without uttering a word.

I later realized that he was dressed in street clothing, not in a bathing suit. I knew then that he wasn't a lifeguard. I don't know who the man was or where he came from, and neither did my sister, but I believe this was my guardian angel, sent to save my life.

After my mother heard what happened, she forbade my sister and me from visiting our cousin unless she was with us. To this day I don't go into bodies of water, as the thought of drowning still haunts me. I can hardly allow water to splash on my face—even while taking a shower—since it makes me feel like I'm suffocating, and the fear of drowning overtakes me.

I was twelve when I experienced my next psychic event. By that time, our village had grown and another family had moved in next to us. They had a girl my age named Muriel, who became another of my friends. However, there was still little for children to do. On long summer days, Muriel and I passed the time lying in the shade watching the clouds slowly drift through the sky. As they floated along, we played a game of spotting the animal figures they made.

One day as we gazed at the sky, I was staring intently at a big billowy cloud when suddenly it opened, revealing a long flight of broad stairs that led up into the center of the cloud. The stairs appeared to be made of marble. A rose-colored hue surrounded the entire scene.

A man stood on one of the stairs, his wife alongside him. They each held the hand of a little girl, who laughed as they helped her jump from stair to stair. The couple smiled as their young son, who was a few steps ahead of them, turned back and waved. A feeling of peace, love, and happiness permeated the scene. I could feel their joy wash over me.

I called out to my friend in amazement, "Look, do you see that?" However, as soon as I spoke those words, the vision dissolved and slowly disappeared. My friend looked but only saw a cloud.

Years later I came to understand that by staring intently at the cloud, I had put myself into a trance and allowed my mind to see into a dimension not normally visible.

The image I saw so overwhelmed me that years later I can still see it in my mind and still feel the love that surrounded the scene.

As a young teenager, I experienced yet another incident. It was a tempestuous day, with a line of storms rolling in one after the other. There was nothing to do except stay inside the house. I sat on the sofa next to my sister, who was engrossed in a book. As she read, I watched her closely, staring at her for a long time. Keeping my eyes on her, I concentrated intently and wondered what it would be like to be her. Suddenly I was leaving my body. Something was rushing up and out through the top of my head and going straight into my sister! All I could think was that I would become a part of my sister and wouldn't be able to return to my own body. Terrified, I began shaking my head back and forth to make the rushing feeling stop. I managed to snap myself out of it, although I felt woozy.

Unlike my other ESP experiences, this one frightened me. The thought of not being able to come back was really terrifying. Even though Joseph later told me that a person's spirit always returns when astral traveling, I never tried leaving my body again. Perhaps it was because of the fear I had felt that no further psychic experiences occurred during my remaining teen years. In fact, nothing more happened until a few years after I married.

Following high school, I studied to become a registered nurse at a teaching hospital in Albany, New York. There I met my future husband, who was completing his medical internship at the hospital. We married young and within five years had four children. During those years, I discovered that my new life was much like the one I had in childhood.

My husband was born and raised overseas in a male-dominated culture. Although he is now 100 percent Americanized in his thinking and mannerisms, at that time it was only natural that he take on the role as head of the household. Having spent his formative years in a culture where men were expected to develop strong, unyielding personalities and have the last word in everything, my husband followed suit and took complete charge of our lives.

I, on the other hand, had grown up learning that a woman's role was to keep her husband happy, and accordingly I did whatever was necessary to keep the peace, including giving in to the wishes and demands of others rather than standing up for what I wanted. Raised to remain unassertive, I kept my thoughts from my husband and relinquished control of my life to him. Consequently I found that in marriage, as in childhood, I had no voice.

However, at that time none of it seemed to matter. I loved my husband dearly and wanted to please him. My only wish was that he would demonstrate his love for me by hugging me or holding my hand. However, my husband wasn't comfortable in showing affection. Little did I realize that I'd chosen a husband to take on the role that my father had played; I once again longed for signs of endearment that were not to come.

After his internship, my husband's medical residencies and fellowship took him from hospital to hospital, so our family moved from one city to another. We moved from Albany to Cleveland to New York City to Youngstown, then on to Boston, followed by West Virginia. Three of the moves found me pregnant and close to delivery. Even so, I packed up our belongings in a U-Haul trailer that we pulled behind us in our 1950 Chevy, and off we went to our next destination.

Life was far from easy. In those days a doctor in training worked long and arduous hours while earning very little money. Many times my husband worked straight through the day and night without a break. Other times he was on duty the entire weekend, leaving Friday morning and returning Monday evening. I spent most of my time with only the children for company.

A doctor pursuing a medical specialty (my husband was studying to become a gastroenterologist) went through one year of internship, three years of residency, and one year of fellowship. Throughout that time, he earned an average of $100 a week—today's equivalent of about $550 a week. Suffice it to say that for a family with three little ones, money was scarce during the early years of our marriage. Not fortunate enough to have a washer and dryer, each night I'd wash diapers by hand and hang them to dry over the shower rod and the playpen. For everything else we depended on weekly trips to a local Laundromat.

Once my husband completed his final year of fellowship in West Virginia, he took a job with a clinic in Marquette, Michigan—quite a distance from upstate New York. I didn't like being that far from home. In particular, I missed my mother. I so looked forward to the long letters that she wrote faithfully each week, telling me all the news from home. By then she had become much more than a mother to me. We'd added a new dimension to our relationship: my mother had become my good friend.

STRANGE OCCURRENCES

W hile living in Marquette, out of loneliness or perhaps boredom now that my children were in school, I rediscovered my interest in psychic phenomena. I longed to know more about extrasensory perception (ESP) and what had happened to me in my youth. Consumed with learning everything possible about ESP, I read as many books on the subject as I could find.

I also tried practicing mind-to-mind telepathy with a friend who shared my interest. Although we faithfully set aside a certain time each day to take turns sending our thoughts to one another, neither of us was able to detect the other's messages. The telepathy didn't work.

I decided to try meditation. To my surprise, I soon found as I closed my eyes and cleared my mind that I began to see certain events before they actually happened. They weren't earth-shattering events—just minor circumstances of personal interest to me. During one of my meditation sessions, I had a vision: I saw a car hit and kill a friend's dog. Along with the vision I saw the image of an empty frame with no picture, and I heard a voice speak in my mind asking me, "Get the picture?" Sadly, a few days later a car hit and killed my friend's dog. Two weeks after that, our dog suffered the same fate. I then understood the meaning of the question that was asked—it was a warning of something to come, which in retrospect I wished that I'd understood and heeded.

Dreams and visions started coming to me as well. In one vision, I saw one of my daughters go flying through a plate-glass panel on a door. At the time we lived in a split-level home with a front door that had two glass panes—a large one on top and a smaller one on the bottom. The door was at the base of the stairs that led from the upper level of the house, where the bedrooms were located.

A few days after the vision, my young daughter came running out of her room, tripped, and fell down the stairs. Her body went completely through the bottom pane of glass. Somehow she wasn't hurt. To my amazement, she did the same thing a second time. After that, I had the glass pane on the bottom section of the door replaced with wood. Thankfully, the accident never reoccurred.

Shortly afterward I began having dreams of future events. In one dream, a neighbor was telling me that our property had the best view of the lake and he wished his family had it. I next heard a voice telling me to consult with a neighbor who, I later learned, was unofficially in charge of settling neighborhood property disputes. Our house in Marquette overlooked Lake Superior, granting us a spectacular view of sailboats and other ships, even large ore boats laden with coal. Soon after my dream, the neighbor who lived next door to us began building an addition onto his house that came suspiciously close to our lot line. Later, as we each worked in our yards, he came over to me and said, "You know your house has the best view of the lake. I wish we had it." It was worded exactly as I had dreamt! Although the addition didn't obscure our view of the lake, after my dream I felt it had to be encroaching on our property.

Instead of following the guidance of my dream and reporting it to the neighbor in charge of disputes, I had a survey of the property done, which allegedly proved me wrong. I knew I should have listened to my dream, but I was reluctant to let anyone know of my visions. I knew I would suffer my husband's wrath if anyone were to find out that I was, as he sarcastically put it, "seeing things." "After all," he'd say, "you are a doctor's wife."

I also tried my hand at automatic writing. It started with an argument between my husband and me. He accused me of insulting his sister, mistaking what he thought he heard me say during a phone conversation. There was no convincing him he was wrong. Saying anything negative about his family was regarded as a serious offense, so my every objection fell on deaf ears. He was determined to make me admit to a wrongdoing and then apologize to him and his sister. Although averse to confrontation and never wanting our children to hear us arguing, I was nevertheless so hurt that my husband didn't believe me that I fought back and maintained my innocence. It was the first time in my married life that I had held my ground and stood up to my husband. This did not sit well. In fact, it developed into days and nights of arguing. Neither of us was about to budge.

Seeking an answer to the situation, I decided to try automatic writing. Sitting quietly before a sheet of blank paper with my eyes closed and pen in hand, I said a prayer for protection and cleared my mind. My hope was to let the spirits guide the pen and deliver a message on the paper. A minute or two later, my little dog that had been lying on the floor beside me started running in circles, barking unceasingly as if something frightening was in the room with us.

Shortly afterward, loud noises, like something banging on sheet metal, began. It was coming from the basement. The banging grew louder. I knew of nothing that could be making those sounds. It was summer so the furnace was off and, with summers in Michigan's Upper Peninsula being cool, there was no need for an air conditioner. Soon the noise became so frightening it scared me into stopping. When I opened my eyes, the banging ceased, as did the dog's barking. I rubbed my eyes, looked around, and saw nothing.

However, on checking the paper, I found a message. The writing in front of me consisted of three words: *error of peer*. Strung together with no breaks or spaces between the words, it looked like this: errorofpeer.

Here was a message from beyond telling me that my husband's accusation was wrong. Just knowing that the spirits agreed with me was enough for me to let go of the argument. I felt that the spirits were of higher authority than my husband.

Naturally I didn't share this experience with him, but I did stop trying to be defensive. Once I stopped fighting, the matter gradually died down and went away.

My husband's financial position slowly but steadily improved. Within a few years we moved from Marquette, Michigan, to Wheaton, Illinois, a western suburb of Chicago. Shortly after we moved, I had another dream. This one was about a child who lived in Marquette and was a friend of my youngest daughter.

While in Marquette, each year I had invited my youngest daughter's friends to our home to bake and decorate Christmas cookies. As we prepared the cookie dough during our last cooking time together, this particular little girl looked at me, smiled shyly, and remarked how much she loved the smell of vanilla. I didn't see her much after that, as she became gravely ill and within months passed away. In my dream she looked at me with that same sweet smile and said, "Please come back to the house with the vanilla-colored walls." Thinking about this sweet child left me so sad that I woke up crying.

A few months later, I experienced a vision like none I had ever before seen. It came to me not in a dream but while fully awake, my eyes wide open. I had just returned from dropping my parents off at O'Hare Airport after a wonderful visit. I sat in the kitchen relaxing with a cup of coffee then looked at the clock and thought to myself, *Good, they're nearly home.* Unlike my father who loved flying, my mother hated to fly. While holding this thought, I glanced over at a cupboard door—and a vision appeared. It showed me an airplane flying along in a sky filled with scattered clouds. As I watched, the plane dropped a few feet and sank slowly into a cloud. At that moment I received an impression that the plane was having trouble. Frightened by the thought that it was the flight my parents were on, I immediately phoned them and was relieved to find out that they were safely home.

I put the vision out of my mind, thinking no more about it until a few months later as I began packing for a family vacation that we were taking to Puerto Rico. The thought suddenly hit me that the plane we would be on just might be the one I had seen in my vision. I tried to convince my husband that we should cancel the trip, though I didn't dare tell him why. [Any time I had mentioned extrasensory perception or dreams or visions, he would silence me, saying he didn't want his children's heads filled with such nonsense.]

With great trepidation, I boarded the plane along with my husband and children. I kept reminding myself that in my vision I hadn't actually seen the plane crash, but only felt that it was having trouble. A couple of hours into the flight I heard an unusual noise, like the powering down of a vacuum cleaner. Then I felt the plane slowly sink a few feet.

Shortly afterward, the pilot came on the intercom to announce that there was a leak in one of the engines and they had shut it down. He assured us that this was not a problem since the plane had three other engines. However, he added, there was a slight change in plans: we would be landing at Miami International airport to make certain everything was in working order. I was certain we would die and it would all be my fault because my vision had given me a warning but I had not let it affect our vacation plans.

The pilot came on again and said that regardless of the price of oil [we were in the midst of a world oil shortage], he was dumping fuel. He added that to conserve energy he was shutting down the air conditioners. It was terrifying to watch the trail of white vapor formed by the discharged fuel as it drifted away on both sides of the plane. Simultaneously, water dripped from the ceiling as the temperature climbed inside the plane.

It seemed to take forever for the plane to descend. When we landed in Miami, I looked out the window and saw that the runway was sprayed with foam, which frightened me even more. The pilot never touched the brakes, rolling the plane to a stop at the terminal gate.

No one debarked. We sat and waited as mechanics went over the plane to locate the problem. Afterward, the pilot came back on the speaker to say they had found the problem—an oil leak. He said the maintenance mechanics had repaired the leak so we could continue. Then the plane took off. When we landed in Puerto Rico, we found our luggage covered in black, greasy streaks, which confirmed the oil leak. After this experience, I began to take my visions more seriously.

Then I had another dream. In this one, a friend of ours was having a heart attack. His face was clearly recognizable. I received the impression he was in pain and reaching out to me for help. When I awoke, I told my husband of the dream. He was skeptical and didn't hesitate to tell me so. Later that day when the phone call came, we learned that what had happened to our friend was exactly as I dreamed. My husband seemed taken aback. However, he explained it away as chance or coincidence.

Months went by before I experienced another extrasensory event. This one, sad and quite eerie, happened on a night when friends invited my husband, his sister, and me to a restaurant for dinner. We were late leaving for the restaurant. We were supposed to meet our friends at 7:00 p.m. and it was already 6:45. The restaurant was a good half hour from our home and it would take even longer to get there due to rush hour. Remembering that I wanted to take something with me to give to my friend, I ran back inside to retrieve it while my husband and his sister impatiently waited for me in the car.

Earlier in the day, our son had called with news that his best friend Bob, a companion from childhood, had just passed away. Bob had spent as much time at our home as his own. He was a part of our family, so my husband and I were shocked and terribly saddened to hear of his passing. Bob had suffered from diabetes from a young age. Recently his blood sugar had spiraled out of control, sending him to the hospital for several days. My son had gone to visit him the night before his release. The next day after the visit, as Bob dressed to go home, he suffered a massive heart attack and died instantly.

I dashed up the stairs to my bedroom and was searching through drawers when suddenly I realized that the air was charged with electricity. I stopped rummaging and stood still. Then, from behind me I clearly heard a voice speaking. A voice I recognized.

It was Bob, and he was addressing me in the same way he always did, saying, "Hey, Miz Emami!"—only this time he was a little louder than usual, as if he were trying to get my attention. Bob always preceded my name with the word "hey" and called me "Miz" Emami. There was no mistaking that this was Bob. It was only natural that he should stop by our house to say good-bye before departing from this earth since our home was like his second home.

I was in shock and couldn't turn around. I regret now that I wasn't able to force myself to face Bob and tell him good-bye. Instead, I said good-bye silently, telling him in my mind how much we would miss him. I'm certain that Bob heard me since, immediately after that, the electricity in the air calmed and the atmosphere returned to normal.

Stunned, I stopped looking for the object that I had forgotten and rushed downstairs to the car. When I told my husband and sister-in-law what had happened, they seemed to believe me—at least, out of respect for the dead, neither of them said a word.

After that experience, I realized that I didn't want such encounters in my life. I don't know if I somehow wished them away or if stopping my practice of meditation had an effect, but after putting thoughts of ESP out of my mind, my paranormal experiences began to fade.

I Make a Change

———

For years my time had been consumed raising my children and doing volunteer work while they were in school. Soon after my youngest child turned sixteen, I realized I'd had my fill of club meetings and bridge matches. I needed a change. I told my husband I wanted to get a job. His response was that I should be happy doing what I was doing, that I had a good life. I persisted, asking him to give me a job in his office so I could gain work experience. When he turned down this request as well, I backed down in the interest of keeping peace.

It was around that time that two new friends came into my life: Carolyn and Sue. When Carolyn and I met, it felt as if we had known each other forever. We talked about many things, including the fact that she, like me, had experienced extrasensory perception. Soon we were sharing our stories.

As for Sue, she and I often had coffee together. One day I mentioned to her that my eldest daughter was having boyfriend trouble. She asked if I had ever thought of taking her to a psychic and proceeded to show me an ad for a psychic fair the following weekend, suggesting we take my daughter. Sue and I went to look it over and to inquire from others which psychic was the best. A very nice woman told us that the star of the show, the one she'd recommend, was Joseph DeLouise. The woman said he seemed a little off that day and guessed it might have been due to the hot weather; nevertheless, she said, he had read for her often and was the only one she recommended.

Later that day, Sue and I returned with my daughter, and Joseph gave her a reading. When it was over, my daughter accused us of giving the psychic information about her. We finally convinced her we hadn't done any such thing and listened as she relayed what Joseph had said. Everything was accurate and on target. He had mentioned, among other things, that her boyfriend was giving her the runaround and also intimated that someone from her past was interested in her. Eventually my daughter broke up with her boyfriend. Soon after, a boy she had dated in high school came back into her life and they began dating. [Today they are happily married and have four wonderful children.]

This reading reignited my interest in psychic phenomena, but first I had to attend to some changes occurring in my life. For one, Sue, Carolyn, and I shared the same discouragement as many mothers of teenagers, feeling as if we were giving a great deal and receiving very little appreciation in return. For another, we wanted to experience something new and different. We tossed around the idea of opening a small breakfast and luncheon restaurant, but our husbands discouraged us, saying we wouldn't be able to make a go of it. Since we didn't have money of our own, without their support we were stuck. Giving up on that idea, Carolyn eventually went to work at her husband's business as the director of human resources, Sue immersed herself in crafts, and I turned to college, where I took a variety of classes, mainly in marketing, secretarial, and office management.

One day while listening to the radio, I heard a discussion about the dyes used in food coloring and a theory that these dyes were causing hyperactivity in children. Recalling that people in the past used beets to color eggs, I decided there must be a better way to make food coloring. Why couldn't it be made from natural foods like fruits and vegetables? Experimenting, I found it worked and the colors were vibrant.

Sue and I together began testing various combinations and came up with beautiful and naturally colored cakes, icing, eggs, and other foods. We tested each recipe twice, baking cake after cake to make certain each color could be replicated. In my husband's opinion, this activity was consuming far too much of my time. He said he was tired of coming home to a messy kitchen and a hastily prepared meal, and wanted me to "put an end to it."

Despite his ranting, I persisted in my efforts. Reflecting on the classes I had taken, I decided I had the skills to turn the recipes into a book and market it through mail order.

After completing the test recipes, Sue and I self-published a book, *Color Me Natural*, and began marketing it through direct mail campaigns, expecting it would generate a lot of money for us. After limited success, we discovered that bookselling wasn't as simple as we thought.

On Meeting Joseph

O ne day Sue spotted an announcement that Joseph DeLouise would be lecturing at a local college. We decided to go and, if given the chance, Sue would ask him about our book. After his presentation, Mr. DeLouise opened the floor to questions. However, he immediately pointed directly at me and said, "Let's start with your question." I gulped and timidly told him my friend and I had written a book, to which he said, "Yes, and you want to know if you will make money."

Knowing we hadn't been successful in our sales effort but not wanting to admit it in front of everyone, I ducked his remark and said, "No, we want to know if you feel a book publisher would be interested in our book." I'm certain he knew what I had done, but he graciously told me that he felt it was possible they would be if the cover were changed. "It isn't effective," he said.

Shortly after that, my feelings about the book took an odd turn. I realized that selling the book had taken a backseat to creating it. Thinking more about the situation, I understood that the important point was having seen the project through to completion rather than the book itself. I had stood my ground and not given in, as was my habit. Somehow I sensed that not only did I need a change but I needed to change myself. To do that, I needed to fight.

Sue and I decided to visit Mr. DeLouise at his office in Chicago. This time we made appointments for a reading for both her daughter and mine. Then on the way to Chicago, we decided to ask him to read for us too, if he had the time.

We must have looked a sorry lot: Sue and I had not done well with book sales, we were dissatisfied with our lives, and both our daughters were having boyfriend trouble. Down in the dumps, we sat in the waiting room uncertain of what lay ahead. When Joseph came out of his office and saw us, he gave us a big, contagious smile, and winked, saying, "I see you have good news for me today." The four of us looked at each other in surprise and then began to laugh. His amusing comment had managed to dissolve our negativity and put us at ease.

A few minutes into my reading, I admitted that I had not been truthful when he had asked me a question about the book during his earlier lecture. I still felt guilty about it, and it showed. He graciously asked me to describe the book. After hearing a little more, he said, "I can tell you how to market your book if you'd like." I thanked him and said I would talk with my friend who had coauthored it.

He then asked to hold an object that belonged to me. I reached into my purse and pulled out my car keys. As he held them, Joseph said, "I see a great deal of energy surrounding you. However, your energy is not directed; it's being spent haphazardly." That sounded like me—spinning my wheels and getting nowhere, not accomplishing a thing. I told Joseph, "I want to make a change, to do more with my life. I want to find out what, if anything else, I am capable of doing."

When the subject of a job came up, I poured out my heart about wanting to work. I found Joseph easy to talk with; he was neither judgmental nor argumentative. I went on to tell him that I was receiving resistance from my husband about working, explaining that he came from a culture where women don't work outside the home and that he was finding ways to discourage me. When I told Joseph that it was causing many arguments, he stopped me, saying, "Its fine to discuss things but don't get into an argument." He told me that having a discussion or a debate is positive, but that arguments and quarrels are negative. Joseph believed that when two people argue, no one wins. "Even when you think you've won, you haven't. You've only made an enemy, and both of you lose," he said.

He advised, "When a conversation starts to get heated, it's best to stop talking and go back to it later, using a different approach. At the beginning it won't be easy, but in time I see your husband coming around and accepting you are working." He added, "One day your husband will even be happy about it." I found that hard to believe, and although I said nothing, I'm sure my face showed my true feelings.

Next, Joseph assured me that everyone on earth had a purpose, and since I was seeking to grow, I should take it as a sign that I was ready to experience more from life. I felt certain he could see my frustration. Then, out of nowhere, Joseph said he had a question for me. He casually asked, "What's the trouble with windmills?" I thought to myself, *Why is he asking me that?* Then, without further thinking, I blurted out, "They only turn one way!" With that, Joseph smiled. [It was years later that I learned why he had asked me about windmills, a conversation that appears later in the chapter "A Gal Friday."]

Joseph moved along, asking me to describe the concerns I had about my children. By the time he finished answering my questions about them, an hour had passed and my session was up.

Following this first reading, I continued to stay in touch with Joseph and went back for another couple of readings. Having another person validate my feelings seemed to spur me on. I told Joseph my fears about being able to compete in the world of work. He stated that he saw many people had played a part in reinforcing my reluctance to speak up, and he assured me I could compete with the best of them, adding that regardless of my doubts he saw me at work.

Laughing, he told me that even if I couldn't believe it, he saw me excelling at my job and moving up quickly. "If you want a job, I will help you get one," he assured me.

A Step Forward

J oseph's confidence in me proved to be infectious. He saw past my reluctance and encouraged me to do the same. So with Joseph's encouragement and his reassurance that hypnosis could help, I decided the time had come to assert myself.

Through hypnosis, Joseph helped me build self-confidence and become assertive. In addition, he gave me down-to-earth advice that helped to reduce my fears and gave me the courage to venture out into the world of work. After each hypnosis session, I left his office feeling that I had something to contribute.

Eventually, in spite of the objections of my husband, I landed a job, as did Sue. She went to work at a craft store, and I started part-time secretarial and data-entry work. I loved being employed and later jumped at the chance to work full time as a secretary. After a couple of years, a sales position opened. I interviewed for it and was given the position on a trial basis. With Joseph's coaching, I soon excelled and became number one in sales. But at home my husband and I argued relentlessly.

Throughout these years I would visit Joseph for hypnosis sessions whenever I felt the need for an extra boost of confidence or wanted to talk through a problem. During one such visit, Joseph helped me understand that I needed to take a share of the responsibility for feeling held back. I'd been telling myself I couldn't do this or that because my husband wouldn't allow it, placing all the blame on him when in reality, as Joseph pointed out, my backing away from doing things was a result of my own fear of failure.

At first it was hard to believe that I created such a problem for myself. The more I thought about it, however, the more sense it made and the more I realized that I was indeed the responsible party. It had been far safer for me to avoid new endeavors than to try them and risk failing. I saw that in avoiding confrontation, I'd set myself up for many of the disappointments I'd experienced. I also came to understand that not facing things head on and getting them out into the open had caused me to act in a passive-aggressive manner, giving my husband reason to complain.

I also found I couldn't entirely blame my husband for the increasing number of arguments we had following my return to work. Pleased to know that people respected my job performance, I became assertive—maybe even a little aggressive. Rather than back down when I didn't agree with my husband, I now began openly disagreeing with him and sometimes even instigating arguments. My newfound confidence propelled me to speak up frequently and express my opinions, all of which took my husband by surprise.

It took a while for my husband to grow accustomed to the new me and for me to realize that we could talk through our differences. Eventually our arguments transformed into discussions, after which things at home began to smooth out and peace prevailed. One evening my husband said he was proud of me and what I had accomplished at my work, words I never thought I would hear from him. Smiling, I remembered what Joseph had told me during our first meeting—that someday my husband would be happy about my working.

Now my husband and I faced life's challenges together, and life certainly presented us with a variety of them. There were happy times—birthdays, family vacations, anniversaries, graduations, our children's marriages, and the many blessings of grandchildren. There were changes as well—moving from one home to another, children going off to college, problems faced by our now-grown children, and difficulties at work that needed to be resolved. There was also illness and hardship, the untimely passing of dearly loved friends, and the death of my husband's parents, followed a few years later by the death of my father. Joseph helped me through my grief on the passing of my dear mother, who had suffered greatly from the devastating cancer that eventually took her life.

Throughout these unsettling events, I visited Joseph, seeking advice and guidance. Over the years, my friendship with Joseph had grown and my visits had become more regular. Now when I visited, we talked about many things, such as our respective circumstances in general, what each of us had done since my last visit, how I was managing at work, how our children were faring. We shared happy times along with disappointments and sorrow. Between visits I would call Joseph to tell him about a sale that I had closed or some other success. It pleased him to hear me speak with confidence.

In 1986, when I discovered Joseph could use some help in his office, I immediately volunteered to assist him on Saturdays. Now that I was well-versed in office work as well as computers, I felt happy to lend a hand.

A GAL FRIDAY

There was never a lack of things to do at Joseph's office. Since he kept everything he needed to know in his head, it soon became clear to me that being organized was not his strong suit, so I became his 'Gal Friday,' doing a bit of everything. I reorganized the office, typed correspondence, set up databases, took notes, and helped tidy up the place.

Then I began stacking copies of articles about his predictions in racks that lined a wall in his outer office, eagerly reading each one. By now he had been published and quoted in a multitude of newspapers and magazines, such as the *Chicago Tribune,* the *Chicago Sun-Times, Chicago Daily News, Reader's Digest, Newsweek, Coronet Magazine, National Enquirer, National Tattler,* the *Wall Street Journal,* and the *Star.* He had also been profiled in the 1975 edition of the *People's Almanac* and *Who's Who in America.*

Several books on the supernatural, which referred to Joseph as a source of psychic research, were stacked on a nearby table. John Godwin honored him in his best-selling novel, *Occult America* published by Doubleday. M.M. Defano noted Joseph in *The Living Prophets,* published by Bernard Geis Associates, and Herbert. B. Greenhouse wrote highly of him in, *Premonitions: A Leap into the Future.*

Also citing Joseph's accomplishments are David Wallechinsky in the *Book of Lists,* Brad Steiger in *Psychic City Chicago* and Hans Holzer in the *Directory of Psychics.* Additionally, *Peoples Almanac 1* and *2* both featured Joseph. He had articles about ESP and his psychic abilities published in *Reader's Digest, Coronet* and *Fate* magazines. The *National Enquirer had* honored him three years in a row.

Behind the racks hung dozens of autographed pictures of celebrities and movie stars for whom Joseph had given personal readings, including Shirley MacLaine, Milton Berle, Jimmy Durante, Burt Reynolds, Joan Rivers, Don Johnson, Liza Minnelli, and many more. I dubbed this Joseph's "Wall of Fame."

Following are some of the photos: Joseph with Merv Griffin, Milton Berle, Jerry Butler, the "Ice Man," Morton Downey Jr., Jimmy Durante, and fellow psychic Jeane Dixon.

Joseph's guest appearance on the Merv Griffin Show in March 1976

Joseph and Milton Berle at a 1970s peace conference

Joseph chatting with the "Ice Man," Jerry Butler

Joseph and Morton Downey Jr. after appearing on Downey's TV show

Joseph and Comedian Jimmy Durante

Joseph DeLousie   Jeane Dixon

PSI '74 CONFERENCES
Psychic/Spiritual/Intuition

Joseph and fellow psychic Jeane Dixon

While filing, I found fascinating newspaper clippings along with many of Joseph's published predictions crammed into a file drawer. These included:

- A copy of the *National Enquirer* dated August 24, 1969, in which Joseph predicted the development of a new type of plastic heart that would render heart transplants unnecessary (The first artificial heart to be successfully implanted in a human was the Jarvik-7, implemented in 1982.)

- A copy of a page from the *People's Almanac* dated January 8, 1969, saying that Chicago psychic Joseph DeLouise predicted Ho Chi Minh would soon die (Ho Chi Minh died that year on September 2 at the age of seventy-nine.)

- An article on Joseph appearing in the *Chicago Sun-Times* edition of January 1, 1978, that included the following predictions:

  o The post office will switch to electric cars in an attempt to economize.

  o A cure for alcoholism will be found.

- A copy of a newspaper article detailing the raging flood of June 9, 1972, in Rapid City, South Dakota, that Joseph had predicted three months earlier, on April 10, while on Bud Miller's program, *PinPoint,* broadcast over Chicago's WLS radio station.

- An article published on September 12, 1969, in *The Prospect Day,* where Joseph predicted a drastic drop in the stock market, named the next elected Illinois governor, and predicted a national wage and price freeze. This article included references to his predictions of the collapse of the Silver Bridge, the Manteno train crash, and the Kennedy-Kopechne drowning tragedy (see figure 3.1).

- An issue of the *Star* dated October 31, 1978, bearing the headline "Psychic Predicted San Diego Jet Disaster 3 Months before It Happened" and recounting how, on June 8, Joseph told Bob Cashen of WAND, an ABC affiliate television station in Decatur, Illinois, the details of a vision he had seen of a midair collision between a jetliner and a private airplane. (The accident, which killed 154 people, happened three months later, on September 25, over the San Diego airport, exactly as Joseph had described it.)

- Headlines in both the *Chicago Tribune* and the *Chicago Sun-Times* mentioning Joseph's predictions regarding the dramatic rise in the price of gold in January 1980.

- Joseph's prediction of Anwar Sadat's assassination printed in "A Seer's Tips for the Year," by James Warren, published in the *Chicago Sun-Times* edition of January 1, 1978 (Anwar Sadat was assassinated on October 6, 1981.)

- The story of Black Monday reported in the *Chicago Tribune* edition of October 19, 1987, the day the stock market nosedived (Joseph had initially made this prediction on the July 26, 1987 Terry Savage financial program *Money Talks* and repeated it on October 11, 1987, in an interview with Mildred Freese of the *Milwaukee Journal.*

The following article by Lois Czubakowski in the *Prospect Day*, details many of Joseph's early predictions:

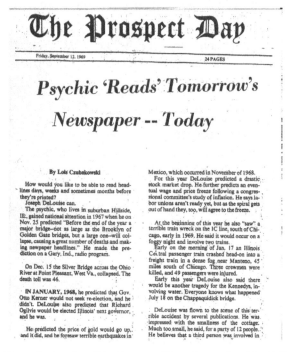

The Prospect Day

Friday, September 12, 1969 — 24 PAGES

Psychic 'Reads' Tomorrow's
Newspaper -- Today

By Lois Czubakowski

How would you like to be able to read head-lines days, weeks and sometimes months before they're printed?

Joseph DeLouise can.

The psychic, who lives in suburban Hillside, Ill., gained national attention in 1967 when he on Nov. 25 predicted "Before the end of the year a major bridge—not as large as the Brooklyn of Golden Gate bridges, but a large one—will collapse, causing a great number of deaths and making newspaper headlines." He made the prediction on a Gary, Ind., radio program.

On Dec. 15 the Silver Bridge across the Ohio River at Point Pleasant, West Va., collapsed. The death toll was 46.

IN JANUARY, 1968, he predicted that Gov. Otto Kerner would not seek re-election, and he didn't. DeLouise also predicted that Richard Ogilvie would be elected Illinois' next governor, and he was.

He predicted the price of gold would go up, and it did, and he foresaw terrible earthquakes in Mexico, which occurred in November of 1968.

For this year DeLouise predicted a drastic stock market drop. He further predicts an eventual wage and price freeze following a congressional committee's study of inflation. He says labor unions aren't ready yet, but as the spiral gets out of hand they, too, will agree to the freeze.

At the beginning of this year he also "saw" a terrible train wreck on the IC line, south of Chicago, early in 1969. He said it would occur on a foggy night and involve two trains.

Early on the morning of Jan. 17 an Illinois Central passenger train crashed head-on into a freight train in a dense fog near Manteno, 45 miles south of Chicago. Three crewmen were killed, and 49 passengers were injured.

Early this year DeLouise also said there would be another tragedy for the Kennedys, involving water. Everyone knows what happened July 18 on the Chappaquidick bridge.

DeLouise was flown to the scene of this terrible accident by several publications. He was impressed with the smallness of the cottage. Much too small, he said, for a party of 12 people. He believes that a third person was involved in

Figure 3. Article in The Prospect Day, *September 12, 1969.*

Also stuffed into drawers were many scraps of paper with clients' handwritten names and addresses. I put them in order, thinking that one day I would enter them into a database.

After cleaning out the drawers, I took it upon myself to set up a new filing system and label the folders. I also answered the phone, made appointments, and typed responses to questions that clients had sent to Joseph. I welcomed clients who came for readings, and personally observed how kindly and honestly Joseph treated each person who came through his door.

Some Saturdays we would let the work wait and just sit and talk. I loved it when Joseph shared his memories with me. He'd talk of his family, his childhood adventures, and his early experiences with ESP, his reluctance to accept he was different from others, the stories behind his amazing predictions, and his visions of the future.

On one such Saturday, the subject of past lives came up. The thought of having a past life fascinated me. My mind immediately filled with lives bursting with excitement, romance, and intrigue. Out of curiosity, I asked Joseph if

118

we had ever been together in another lifetime. Joseph smiled, leaned back in his chair, eyes half-closed, and replied, "Yes, we've come back together several times." He added that during my initial reading with him, he recognized me from a past life. "When I looked, I saw you dressed in clothing from years gone by. You were wearing an old-fashioned long dress and a bonnet tied beneath your chin. We lived on a farm then, and you complained each time the wind changed direction and the windmill stopped turning. I finally put up a second windmill, right next to the original one, only facing in a different direction. We then had continually turning windmills whenever the wind was blowing, no matter what the direction. That day in my office when you answered, 'Windmills only turn one way,' it confirmed for me that it really was you from a past lifetime."

Hearing this made me laugh and, of course, doubly happy that I had volunteered to help Joseph in his office. I felt I was destined to be here.

Joseph went on to say that in one lifetime we were married and had three children. We were affluent, owning a large farm and employing several laborers. However, the times were turbulent: war was brewing. Joseph was a peacemaker in that lifetime, negotiating with both sides in an attempt to stave off war. "But," he said solemnly, "I failed."

He told me: "Early one morning, we awoke to the sound of muffled footsteps. We looked out a window to discover the sounds came from marching soldiers. They were stopped right outside our home, poised to attack. Quickly gathering our children from their beds, we fled through the fields, cannonballs exploding all around us."

Lowering his voice, Joseph continued. "During another lifetime we were pirates. I was a young buccaneer, barely fifteen. You were older, and since I was new to bootlegging and plundering, you took me under your wing and taught me the art of sword fighting. I fought bravely, knowing I had the assurance you would watch out for me. Things went as planned, and we fought side by side, winning many a battle—until one day we were outnumbered and our ship was nearly overtaken. In the heat of battle, we became separated."

Joseph sighed, pausing briefly. After a moment he added, "I was looking across the bow to find you, when suddenly a sailor's sword sliced through my body. Our eyes met as I slumped to the floor. I heard you shout, 'No!' and saw the horror on your face as you watched me die."

Hearing this, I was overcome with sadness and not at all eager to hear more.

Nevertheless, Joseph went on, saying, "We were briefly together in another lifetime as part of a royal court."

My eyes lit up. Surely, *this* would be a good story.

Joseph saw my excitement and quickly added, "It's not what you're thinking. We weren't among the elite members of court. Our ties with royalty were more along the line of 'kept people.' I was a court jester; you were a harem dancer. We were there for the king's entertainment."

Joseph recounted, "I was entranced with you, and you shared my feelings, smiling and flirting each time you saw me. I had a hard time taking my eyes off you even while I was on stage and should have been concentrating on how the king was reacting to my performance.

"The distraction proved fatal. Displeased with my act, the king was swift in giving the order, 'Off with his head!' The last thing I remember was your scream and the thud when my head hit the floor."

I shuddered and gasped. Joseph sat up and looked me straight in the eyes, a smile dancing across his face. The thought crossed my mind that Joseph might be flirting with me. There was an awkward moment of silence, and then the phone rang.

I was glad for the break. I didn't know what Joseph's intentions were, but I definitely knew mine. I'd thought that hearing about past lives would be fun, but after learning the outcome of ours, any fantasies I had were quickly dispelled. I wasn't about to tempt fate this time around.

I excused myself early. With that, the door to revelations of past lives was closed. The next time I saw Joseph, things were back to normal and our regular routine continued. Never again was the subject of past lives brought up.

Once I finished rearranging the office, I began to help Joseph create publicity pieces. Later I wrote news releases of his predictions in an effort to increase his media exposure. I also researched radio and television talk programs and generated a list of new media contacts.

One Saturday I discovered that my duties were not to be purely administrative. For the first time, I was to witness Joseph at work while in trance. Joseph was experimenting with his gift, pushing the envelope. Prior to entering a trance, Joseph explained to me some of the things that might happen.

First, he warned me that sometimes a vision of a future event would leap into his mind when he was not meditating and put him into a trancelike state. He said this was a challenge, as it could hit him wherever he was, no matter what he was doing. He told me he had no control over it and that the experience always left him disoriented.

He said even when a trance was self-induced, it would usually take him a minute or two to clear his mind on coming out of it but not to worry, that soon he would be in the present again.

Next Joseph explained that when he was shown a vision, it was important for him to base his interpretation on the feelings that came through rather than trying to apply logic. He said if he tried to intellectualize what he was shown, the message could be misinterpreted or the vision might completely stop.

I was very interested in his trance states, and when I sat next to him taking notes, I noticed certain peculiarities. When Joseph put himself into a trance, the air around us began to change—it started to tingle. As the tingling intensified, my forehead, starting at the center and spreading outward, tightened and then knotted. I found myself unable to relax the entire time Joseph was in trance. Throughout, Joseph emitted an energy that charged the atmosphere and for some reason kept my forehead taut until he came out of trance.

Unbeknownst to Joseph, I had experienced this energy many years before, when my daughter, my friend Sue, and I had attended one of his lectures. As was his habit, Joseph stayed around after his talk to answer questions. I approached him and asked if he went into a trance when he gave a psychic reading. He took my hand, smiled at me, and asked, "Do you mean like this?" He tilted his head back and seemed a little unsteady on his feet as his eyes rolled up into their sockets. Seeing the whites of his eyes and fearing he might fall or pass out, I kept hold of his hand. After a few moments he opened his eyes, smiled again, and said, "Yes, sometimes I do."

I laughed, thanked him, and we walked away. Within five minutes, my hand began to feel warm. Glancing down at the back of my hand, I could see a red line extending from the base of my ring finger halfway to my wrist. I was astounded. During the nearly half hour it took for the line to fade, I kept thinking that Joseph must emit some type of energy.

Not until I began working with Joseph did I discover that I had been correct in my thinking. At that point, the energy Joseph emitted when he went into trance was knotting my forehead.

I've never experienced this energy transmission with any other psychic I have visited.

Another peculiarity I noticed while working with Joseph was that although he could slip into a trance in a matter of moments, in order to get a clear picture of the visions he required a deep period of extended concentration. Sadly, he often lacked sufficient time for this. Work kept us busy.

Once I had the office in order, it was time to go electronic. When I asked for a computer, Joseph immediately bought one. As soon as it was installed, I began typing and electronically storing the myriad notes and articles I'd found.

One day when I walked into the office, Joseph surprised me by showing me a website he'd commissioned for his business.

Moving 'full steam ahead' into the electronic age, he learned to use MS Word and navigate the Internet. Joseph thoroughly enjoyed this new knowledge, and, with a completely modernized office, I was pleased that everything was finally up to date.

MARILYN MONROE

After Joseph's newly organized office was quiet, we would sit and talk. Although Joseph never revealed information about people who were living, he did not mind talking of the dead, and I certainly did not mind listening. Some of our most interesting conversations involved his friendship with Marilyn Monroe, one of his first clients, who had become a friend.

Hanging on a wall in his inner office, separate from his "wall of fame," was a personally autographed pinup of Marilyn that she gave Joseph in appreciation for his advice.

Joseph had known Marilyn for a long time. He first met her when a friend of hers [who frequented his beauty shop] had put them in touch. Then while visiting California in 1959, Joseph read for Marilyn. She valued his advice and continued to consult him over the years, calling him every four or five months to ask him about one man or another whom she'd recently met—what would he be like? Did he love her? Would they marry? Would she have children? She asked as well about her ambitions in the movie world. Joseph and Marilyn had a total of at least twelve conversations.

There are some people whose paths are meant to cross, and this was true of Joseph and Marilyn. Marilyn valued Joseph's guidance and looked upon him as a friend and confidant. From the beginning, Joseph felt that she needed his guidance more than a psychic knowledge of her future. Having observed that she was scattered and impatient in striving to achieve too many goals at once, he advised her to focus on her efforts one at a time. He also saw that she had the ambition and drive to succeed in Hollywood and in life, but her impatience for success often led her to make hasty decisions.

Marilyn had suffered abuse both throughout her childhood and in her later years. Often deceived by untrustworthy people, near the end of her life she found herself in a situation that left her unable to control the outcome. On August 3, 1962, Marilyn phoned Joseph. As soon as she began to speak, he could see her life was in jeopardy. She was furious, yelling about getting even with the "SOBs" who were following her and trying to bribe her to keep quiet. "But I won't!"

she screamed. "I'm going to get even with all of them!" She threatened to "spill her guts, blow the whistle, tell all she knew" about those who had broken their promises to her. She was distraught—angry with certain high-ranking people she knew well. "They're nothing but bastards!" she screamed into the phone. She told Joseph that those she thought loved her had betrayed her, used her. She insisted she was out to expose them, to tell everyone confidences they had shared with her, including that they were planning to run Robert Kennedy for president.

Warning lights flashed through Joseph's mind. He saw that Marilyn knew too much. Too many people around her who liked to brag about their endeavors were talking about covert things. Joseph warned Marilyn to get away, to "pack a suitcase and take a vacation until things calm down." He kept her on the phone, letting her vent as he repeatedly cautioned her to stop talking about these matters since she was putting herself in danger.

However, Marilyn was listening to no one. Again, Joseph urged her to leave town and stop talking. But no matter how often he warned her about the perilous situation she was in, she wouldn't listen. Three days later, on the morning of August 6, 1962, Joseph heard the news of Marilyn Monroe's so-called suicide the night before.

Not until October 15, 2002, during the fortieth anniversary year of Marilyn Monroe's death, did Joseph publicly reveal his impressions of her death. As a guest on the cable television program *River West Flowing,* hosted by Cynthia Austin, he told Austin he was there not to commemorate Marilyn's death but to talk about what had happened. He said, "Although Marilyn is in the spirit world, the lies about killing herself are holding her back from growing. She wants people to know that she did not kill herself. Marilyn wants the truth to come out."[1]

He went on to describe how he had met Marilyn in 1959, conducted a reading, and drawn up an astrological chart for her. Her chart indicated that she was stubborn, ambitious, and destined for fame. Joseph said: "Marilyn could be nasty—she started to believe in her own image. The studios tried to change her, but she didn't want to change. She liked herself and was studying to become a serious actor, taking acting lessons. Marilyn made it the easy way because of her beauty."[2]

Joseph related how, a couple of weeks before her death, Marilyn had called and confided in him about the people with whom she was friendly—people in politics, the movie industry, the government, and syndicated crime. Joseph said: "She often entertained at Hoffa's parties. She knew a lot of people; they all loved her. Marilyn talked of Peter Lawford, John Kennedy, and Robert Kennedy. Robert was the last one she was seeing." Joseph added, "She was obsessively in love with Robert. They were very compatible."[3]

Marilyn had told Joseph that Robert broke promises he'd made to her. When Joseph tried to explain that Robert wasn't in a position to make good on his promises, that perhaps she was "sort of being used," Marilyn screamed at him and hung up.

Joseph continued his conversation with Cynthia Austin, relating details of the last conversation that he and Marilyn had on August 3, 1962, two days before her death. "Marilyn was furious, claiming that Robert was not accepting her phone calls. Irate, she claimed she was going to "spill her guts, blow the whistle, and tell all she knew."

Joseph went on, "Marilyn was threatening to expose everything. It was obvious she knew too much about organized crime, politics, the CIA, and the FBI.

"I warned her, 'Marilyn, get out of there. Keep quiet; stop talking.'"[4]

At this point Austin asked, "Joseph, why have you waited forty years to talk about this?"

Joseph replied that he had become involved with other work—the Helen Brach murder, the Sharon Tate murders, the Zodiac Killer, and building his practice. Only in 1997, when he had been hospitalized for a quadruple bypass, did the issue of Marilyn's death resurface.

He explained that while he was on the operating table, he flatlined and had an out-of-body experience. "It was when I was close to death that fifty years of experiences rushed into my mind, Marilyn's death being one of them. Later, lying in my hospital bed, I began thinking about Marilyn and asked myself, 'Why am I waiting?'"

Joseph paused then pointed out, "In the months following my recovery I began holding séances, going into trance and contacting Marilyn. Each time she came through, she would emphasize, 'Pills did not kill, pills did not kill, pills did not kill!'"

He elaborated, "It was a contract murder. It wasn't a peaceful death like when you take pills and slip away. It was a violent death—she fought against her killers."

"It wasn't suicide. Nothing was sectioned off—the linens were washed, everything was cleaned up. Where were the police cordoning off [the crime scene], preserving evidence? This was a nasty way to die. She was tranquilized, subdued, and then given drugs."

Joseph said he saw that Marilyn fought against the men who were holding her down—fought until the tranquilizer overpowered her and she could fight no longer. "It was murder," he declared.[5]

"It's hard to think she had to be put away," Joseph asserted.

Surprised at this remark, Austin asked, "Do you mean that she didn't have to die?"

Joseph explained, "People involved in politics needed to silence her. They were forced. If she had talked, it would have been a national risk. It was covered up. It's not like today. You couldn't get away with it today. The media would be all over it. Back then, the pathologist, the chief of police, and the maid—everyone who was involved—couldn't talk. If they talked, their lives would be in danger."

Joseph then disclosed, "My life was threatened as well. Marilyn kept a diary in which she had written my name and phone number as well as the things we talked about during our conversations. They must have found it. On August 8, 1962, I received a phone call from a man who, in a menacing voice, warned me, 'We know that you talked with Marilyn. It would be wise for you not to say anything.'"

Joseph explained, "At the time I had six children to support, so I said nothing. I grew up on the near north side of Chicago—I know a threat when I hear one.

I've kept quite all these years, and now it's my intention to let people know what really happened—that Marilyn did not kill herself; she did not take any pills."[6]

PART IV
LATER PREDICTIONS

OUT OF THE CORNFIELDS

In June of 1989, Joseph made public a prediction of a plane crash that would end in an unexpected tale of survival. He was on Cliff Kelly's WVON Chicago radio program, broadcast from Chicago and heard in Indiana, Wisconsin, and neighboring Chicago suburbs. Following a discussion about Joseph's previous predictions, Cliff asked Joseph if he would offer the audience any new predictions he had.

Listening to the show from my home in suburban Chicago, I knew what Joseph was going to say. I was with him in his office the month before when this horrendous vision came to him. It was not often that I was with Joseph when a vision of this magnitude came through, and it was shocking to witness. As Joseph slowly leaned back in his chair and closed his eyes, I waited, pen in hand, ready to take notes. In a matter of minutes he looked peaceful and relaxed. Then, as his concentration deepened, he suddenly began to tremble. It wasn't long before his whole body was shaking. I grew anxious. I had never before seen anything like this happen.

I thought about bringing him out of his trance but hesitated, not knowing how he would react. Just then Joseph began to speak and I took the following notes: "I see a plane. It's coming in fast—trying to land, but something's wrong. It's wobbling, out of control. It's down now, and there's a fire. I see people walking away from the crash. I see them—they're walking out of cornfields."

As Joseph slowly began to return to a normal state of consciousness, he was mumbling. He was shaken and seemed a little woozy, as if still under and not fully awake. I didn't know whether to talk or remain quiet. I was eager to find out if he was all right but didn't want to do harm by bringing him around too soon.

I decided to see if Joseph would begin speaking clearly on his own. Gradually he came to and, after a few minutes, he repeated to me what he had seen. As soon as he finished, I jumped up to prepare a news release. But Joseph stopped me before I could turn on the computer, saying he didn't want to share this information just yet.

Joseph decided to wait until his next radio appearance before making this prediction public. Radio hosts at this time checked in with him on a regular basis to see if he had anything new to share, so we knew it would not be long before another opportunity presented itself. Sure enough, a few weeks later Cliff Kelly invited Joseph to be a guest on his show in June.

During the broadcast, Joseph gave his new prediction. He told Cliff, "I see a large passenger plane coming in for a landing. The plane's in trouble. It's approaching fast, having difficulty staying on course. It's wobbling, as if out of control."

Joseph continued, "There's a crash, an explosion—a fire. I see people. They're walking out from cornfields."

Cliff interrupted. "Wait, Joseph," he said. "Hold on. You know people don't survive large plane crashes."

Joseph replied, "I know, but this is what I see. I see many people surviving this crash, walking out from the cornfields."

He went on to say, "I feel it will happen soon and that the crash will take place in the Midwest."[1]

What Joseph had foreseen was United Airlines Flight 232—a DC-10 with 297 people on board—that crash-landed a few weeks later, on July 19, 1989, in Sioux City, Iowa. After its rear engine exploded and shrapnel tore through the plane's hydraulics lines, Captain Al Haynes and the crew struggled to control the malfunctioning plane. Miraculously, they made it to the airport.

When the plane hit the runway, it somersaulted, broke into pieces, and burst into flames. A large section of the airliner landed in cornfields adjoining the airport.

Altogether, of the 297 aboard, 113 lost their lives. Captain Haynes survived because, during the crash landing, the nose of the airplane buried itself in the ground.

Unbelievably, 183 people survived, many of whom walked out from the cornfields as Joseph had seen. Some were badly hurt; others barely suffered a scratch.

FORESEEING DEATH:
PRINCESS DIANA

⟢━━━━⟣

In 1997, *Who's Who in America* named Joseph one of the country's outstanding clairvoyants. In September of that same year, *American Woman Magazine* named him one of the country's top ten psychics. Through my work with Joseph, I knew both of these accolades were well deserved. The longer I worked with him, the more impressed I was with the way he interacted with people.

He was honest and trustworthy, practiced what he preached, and exhibited an upbeat approach to life that he hoped others would adopt. He had a great sense of humor and laughed easily at himself. In addition, Joseph was true to his word. I never knew him to lay claim to a prediction that he had not publicly documented prior to its occurrence.

There were, however, some visions that Joseph did not make public. Here, I offer one such vision about Princess Diana as testament to the honor of his word. This particular vision came to Joseph around the middle of August 1997 when he was not feeling well enough to put himself into a trance state. Nevertheless, he was unable to stop this vision from coming.

As he leaned back in his chair intending to rest, he softly spoke the following words—which I recorded:

"I see a funeral procession winding its way slowly down the streets of London. It's a royal procession. Mourners are lining the streets. Throngs of people are grieving and crying as the procession passes by.

"There are bouquets after bouquets of flowers, thousands of them. Their perfume hangs in the air. The fragrance is overwhelming.

"Everywhere I look there are flowers—they're lying on sidewalks, on lawns, and woven into fences. They cover every available space.

"There's a sea of flowers. They're everywhere I look."

A member of the royal family had died, but Joseph did not know which member. He had seen a coffin in his vision, but it was closed so he could not see whose body it held.

Since the Queen Mother was elderly, I thought she was most likely the one who had passed. Joseph did not make any such assumption, however, insisting he did not know who it was.

I thought we should put out a news release, but Joseph stopped me. He felt the event was destined to happen soon and he was scheduled for bypass surgery. Joseph knew he would be too weak to take on a deluge of reporters.

It turned out that he had envisioned the funeral procession of Princess Diana, who was killed in a car accident in Paris two weeks later on August 31, 1997, when the driver of her limo raced to escape the paparazzi.

On news of her death, grieving mourners blanketed the sidewalks with multitudes of flower bouquets, laid down in memory of their beloved Princess.

It's good that Joseph prevented me from publishing a news release. A few days after Diana's death, he had his quadruple bypass. After his surgery the doctors were not able to close Joseph's chest immediately, since they were having trouble restarting his heart, a situation they referred to as "lazy heart." They weren't able to take Joseph off the life-support machines until his heart resumed beating on its own. After the third attempt and a disconcerting amount of time, Joseph's heart finally responded. This and additional complications following the surgery kept Joseph in critical condition for two weeks, during which time he came close to death several times.

Amy Lauer, public relations specialist who had worked for Joseph for many years and "adopted" him as a father, stayed with him throughout the long ordeal. When Joseph was in intensive care, she slept in a chair in the lobby. When he was transferred to a regular hospital room, she spent each night watching over him, sleeping on a cot in the room. Later Joseph told me that he would never have pulled through had it not been for Amy's constant vigil.

Amy had long been important to Joseph. Gifted with a wonderful writing style—partly perhaps because of her heritage as a descendant of Edgar Allan Poe—she wrote many excellent publicity pieces and articles, as well as beautiful poems.

Joseph had introduced Amy to her future husband David, a man who had come to him for advice on moving up in his career. Seeing that David's job would lead nowhere, Joseph told him he could help him break into financial advising. He coached David on the ins and outs of the stock market and taught him to spot financial trends. When appearing as a guest on programs that featured finance and stocks, Joseph sometimes invited David to speak on the market and the future of certain stocks. Thanks to Joseph, David became a successful and well-established financial advisor.

From the moment they met, David was smitten with Amy. He loved that she was vivacious and full of life. Once he secured his future, it didn't take long for him to ask for her hand in marriage.

Like Amy, David also grew close to Joseph. He and Amy were there whenever Joseph needed help. For instance, Joseph suffered from type 2, adult-onset diabetes. Although he watched his diet carefully and was vigilant about his insulin regime, at times his diabetes became brittle. The resulting drop in his blood sugar could easily send him into a diabetic coma, and it was impossible to predict when the next episode would occur. More than once Amy and David came to Joseph's rescue, often very late at night.

At the time, Joseph was living alone. He and his third wife, Sonja, had separated two years before. While Joseph never went into detail about their separation, it was my feeling that Joseph's strange affinity for solitude was a factor. Worried about Joseph living by himself, Amy and David insisted that Joseph come live with them immediately after their wedding. Thank goodness they did, for it was within months of moving into their home that Joseph discovered his need for bypass surgery.

Following his heart operation, Joseph told me of a spiritual event he experienced during the surgery. When the doctors first attempted to restart his heart, he suddenly found himself standing at one end of the operating table observing the procedure. From there he watched the doctors' second unsuccessful attempt to restart his heart. He could see the look of worry in the doctors' eyes as they glanced nervously at one another.

At that moment, Joseph looked up and saw flocks of tiny angels descending from above. Cherubs—the angels closest to God's throne—swarmed around the operating table, while dozens of cherubim enveloped and supported his still body. Joseph saw they also were inside his head. Some of the angels were working on his mind, pushing out doubt and fear. Suddenly, fifty years of life flashed before his eyes in what seemed like seconds, flooding him with long-forgotten memories.

As he continued to observe himself on the operating table, other cherubs fluttered around, passing through the hands of the doctors and nurses.

The angels remained with Joseph as the doctors shocked his heart a third time. Finally, his heart resumed beating on its own.

It was then that Joseph felt himself sliding back into his body. As he did, the words *Not yet, Joseph...not yet* echoed faintly in his head.

PREDICTIONS OF 9/11

S eptember 11, 2001, will forever be remembered as the day terrorists sent two passenger planes crashing into the Twin Towers of the World Trade Center, a third plane into the Pentagon, and a fourth—United Airlines Flight 93—plummeting into the tranquil countryside of Pennsylvania. It is believed that the plane that crashed into the Pentagon was targeted to crash and bomb the White House. United Flight 93 was planned as a backup should the first plane fail in its mission. But, in fact, both planes failed. The first missed the White House due to an error made by the novice pilot; the second failed due to the American heroes aboard United Flight 93.

On January 11, 1999, more than two and a half years before the fateful 9/11 event, Joseph was a featured guest on the popular internationally broadcast *Coast to Coast AM* radio program hosted by Art Bell. Around 3:30 in the morning, Joseph made a startling prediction concerning a plane crash, which he repeated again early in 2001 on Cliff Kelly's WVON Chicago radio show.

That night in 1999, I was listening to Art Bell's program along with a world-wide audience of several thousand. Joseph came on during the second hour of the show. He spoke about crystals and the amazing properties they contain. He and Art conversed about spirits and ghosts, possession and exorcism, aliens and flying saucers, and other psychic phenomena. Bell seemed startled when Joseph told him that people who see UFOs are "wired-in," that there is some sort of connection.

The talk moved on to movie stars for whom Joseph had given psychic readings. They then spoke of Joseph's many guest appearances on television and radio, mentioning several of the celebrity hosts who had invited him to appear on their shows, such as Johnny Carson, Merv Griffin, David Susskind, Morton Downey Jr., and Chicago's longtime columnists and television hosts Irv Kupcinet of Channel 11 and Terry Savage of CBS. Joseph and Art talked for nearly two hours.

As I well knew, Joseph could talk all night. He loved interacting with people, and the topic of paranormal events was second nature to him. Their conversation soon turned to mind power and the power of prayer and how collective prayers from a like-minded group could bring about change. Joseph mentioned an article he had written for *Coronet Magazine* entitled "It's All in Your Mind." In it, he discussed how the power of the mind can accomplish things and allow you to see what others might not.

Just before a station break in the wee hours of that wintry morning, Bell asked Joseph if he would meditate during the break and give his listening audience a new prediction for the future, one that would be heard for the first time on his show. Aware that there would only be a few short minutes for him to "see" a future event, Joseph realized that time might be an issue. Normally before appearing on a radio show, Joseph would enter a trance a few days ahead of time in order to have a prediction ready. But Art Bell had invited him to be on the show that morning, and he had spent the day putting together notes for the interview.

Joseph later told me that during the station break he stilled his mind, leaned his head back, closed his eyes, and, concentrating inwardly, waited patiently for a vision. It didn't take long. Within minutes he became jittery and knew he was about to receive an important vision—one that he wouldn't look forward to either seeing or revealing.

Back on the air, Joseph opened his eyes and brought his head upright. Art was asking him if he had seen anything that would be of interest to his audience. Was there anything he wanted to share?

The first thing Joseph told Art was that he saw a volcano erupting at the very moment he relaxed his mind. Bell wasn't the least bit impressed, telling Joseph that wasn't what he'd call a prediction—that volcanoes erupt all the time.

Without hesitating Joseph continued, giving Art and his audience a real blockbuster of a prediction. Listeners around the world were stunned when Joseph told Bell he saw that terrorists were going to bomb the White House. "Don't worry," he said, "they're going to miss; the bomb will hit somewhere else, somewhere near the grounds of the White House." Joseph told Art that he felt the terrorists might launch a missile from a semitrailer truck parked in a secluded area miles from the White House.[2]

The phones began ringing, and Bell moved quickly to accept calls from his audience. The calls took up the remaining time.

A few days after the *Coast to Coast* broadcast, Joseph received a phone call from a man who identified himself as FBI, cautioning him to stop talking about threats on the White House and not to make any further predictions about terrorist activities. Others contacted Joseph as well, including worried clients who'd heard him on the radio and wanted to know what else he saw.

Shortly thereafter, Joseph once again entered into a trance to focus further on the fatal vision. I was present at this second sitting, which brought Joseph the following additional insights that he subsequently revealed to audiences on other talk shows.

Joseph saw six terrorists gathered at a meeting in Malaysia discussing plans for bringing down the United States. His expanded vision opened with all six terrorists shouting at the same time, arguing about how to carry out the attack.

When he first received the vision on Art Bell's show, Joseph learned that the terrorists were planning to shoot a missile from a semitrailer truck parked in a secluded spot miles away from the White House. During the second sitting, Joseph saw the terrorists arguing about whether firing a missile was in fact the best method of attack. Some argued that a plane loaded with fuel would make a far more effective and devastating "bomb."

Joseph picked up other differences of opinion as well. While a number of the terrorists held the view that it would be best to strike the White House first, others believed it would make a stronger statement to hit the Twin Towers since these buildings housed international finance offices. Those in favor of first striking the White House viewed it as destroying the seat of American imperialism. As we now know, it turned out that those who voted to first hit the Twin Towers prevailed, and on September 11, 2001, the terrorists carried out their horrific plan.

In the days following 9/11, Joseph cleared his mind and centered further on the horrendous tragedy. His expanded vision showed him that the plane hitting the Pentagon was originally slated to bomb the White House; however, the pilot, a novice, was unfamiliar with the terrain and unable to identify his target. The White House was obscured by trees, and he overshot it. Discovering his error, the pilot picked the next most crucial target within his view—easily identifiable from the air—and dove straight into the Pentagon. United Flight 93, the hijacked plane that crashed into the Pennsylvania countryside as brave passengers fought to regain control, was also headed for Washington. It was part of the terrorists' backup plan in the event the other plane should fail to hit the White House.

After the 9/11 bombings, eyewitnesses to the Pentagon disaster claimed a missile rather than a Boeing 757 had hit the building. Joseph disagreed with this theory, even though it would have lent more credibility to his original prediction—that there was to be a missile fired at the White House. He was certain an airplane had hit the Pentagon.

Joseph had a talent for getting directly to the heart of a matter. Over the years he had found a need to relate events in a clear and concise way to make it easy for people to envision what he had seen. With this in mind, Joseph portrayed the terrorists' error in this way: "The terrorists made a major mistake on 9/11. The mistake they made was first hitting the 'lungs' of the country [the Twin Towers] before they hit the 'heart' [the White House.]" He said it would have caused far greater confusion and done far more psychological damage had they first hit the country's heart and then hit the lungs.

When Joseph publicly said he could hear the terrorists arguing about how to carry out the attack, he was asked how he was able to understand what the terrorists were saying since they were speaking another language. To this he replied, "Perceived information is impressed upon the mind without words being spoken. Thoughts, feelings, and emotions are translated into words—silent words that are 'heard' in the mind." Joseph went on to explain that it wasn't necessary for him to physically hear words, since psychic communication is telepathic. "To picture how it works, think of a mind reader receiving thoughts—no words are spoken. The mind reader mentally receives thoughts from the mind of another person. Now picture a medium telepathically receiving thought. Through thought transference, a medium mentally receives thoughts from the mind of spirit."

THE ANTHRAX SCARE

A fter the attempted bombing of the White House on September 11, 2001, Joseph received dozens of requests concerning the anthrax scare that was holding the country in a grip of fear. Anonymous letters laced with deadly anthrax spores had begun arriving at media companies and congressional offices, the first of which had been mailed on September 18. Such letters were discovered every couple of days from October through November, their contents testing positive for anthrax poisoning, resulting in five deaths and seventeen infections.

The FBI had begun to investigate the mail incidents on October 9, announcing a public request for information that might lead to the arrest of the perpetrators. After many calls from nervous Americans eager to have the case solved, Joseph stilled his mind and entered a trance. He then outlined the psychic impressions he received in a letter which I typed. The letter, which was sent to the FBI, read:

DATE: November 10, 2001

SUBJECT: Anthrax Lead

TO: FBI

FROM: Joseph DeLouise

Chicago Clairvoyant

After the attempted bombing of the White House on September 11, which I foresaw and predicted on the January 11, 1999 Art Bell *Coast to Coast* radio program, I received dozens of requests from his audience to meditate on the anthrax scare to help solve the case and catch the perpetrators.

Upon psychically meditating, I received the following impressions, which I am submitting upon the FBI's request asking for information leading to the arrest and conviction of those people guilty of this act.

My psychic impressions are:

There are 4 people involved in this crime: one woman and three men. The main person responsible is a Vietnam veteran that was a helicopter pilot in the war. He is in his middle 50's, has a receding hairline, brownish colored hair, 5'10," about 185 pounds. He has a tattoo of his Vietnam Company name and number on his arm. He was wounded in the war. His name starts with an *R*.

He has a grudge of some kind against the government and politicians or possibly against the *National Enquirer* where at one time he worked as a writer. The anthrax was targeted to hit politicians and the media; the others infected were accidental. The woman, whose name begins with an *A*, has a rough personality and loves sailing. The other two men are younger. One of them is about 35 to 40, is short and stocky with a beard. He knows about chemistry and germs. The anthrax was stolen from a research center that the younger man had access to.

The sloped handwriting on the envelope was a deliberate disguise as well as one of the words in the letter being misspelled on purpose to throw you off the track. I foresee one of those involved will blow the whistle for the reward money, which I feel should be upped to 5 million dollars to entice him to come forward.

They operate from a cruise ship off the coast of Florida that travels back and forth to the Caribbean. The boat's name starts with SEA. It is SEA ____ ____. The rest of the name has something to do with a sea monster, or a sea serpent or a sea scorpion—it seems that there is a mythical name involved.

Whether or not the letter was of assistance to the FBI is unknown as Joseph never received a response.

LATER TELEVISION APPEARANCES

- In December 1993, on the Chicago television program *On Call* hosted by Marilyn Spanos of Multi Media TV, Joseph predicted

  o A scandal surrounding President Bill Clinton.

  o Michael Jordan returning to basketball. (Jordan had abruptly retired during the 1993–1994 season then rejoined the Bulls in 1995.)

  o The Soviet Union would enter into conflict with surrounding countries that would return to the Soviet Union as socialists, not communists.

  o The cardinals at the Vatican would vote in a very liberal pope.

- In June 2001 on Mark Sims's television show *View Point,* Joseph predicted that a large plane would be going down soon—"a big one, big like a B-1 bomber."[3] [On November 12, 2001, American Airbus 587 took off from New York and crashed in Queens, killing 251 passengers, 9 crew, and 5 on the ground.]

- In 2001 while on Chicago's Channel 19's television program *River West Flowing* hosted by Cynthia Austin and Leonard Grady,[4] Joseph predicted that

  o We're heading for a police state—"possibly a sort of dictatorship."

  o In fifty years there would be world population control. He said that a chemical to prevent births would be put in the water. "Women will need to register to get a child and will be given an antidote to get pregnant."

- In 2003, on Chicago's TV Channel 9, Joseph predicted that marijuana would be legalized and that peace will come to the Middle East. "But these things," he asserted, "will take time."[5]

- In 2005, when the host who was to interview Joseph on Channel 19's *River West Flowing* failed to show up, Joseph self-hosted the show. In his presentation he included the following events which he foresaw materializing in the future:

  o China will make a grab for South America.

  o In fifty years there will be a United South America.

  o Gasoline prices will increase to five dollars a gallon.

  o Oil prices will rise to fifty dollars a barrel, then ninety dollars a barrel and higher.

  o A real estate bust lies ahead for the United States.

  o There will be sales of human organs for transplants going to the highest bidder, with most organs coming from China.

  o Life will be discovered on Mars.

  o The United States is heading toward socialism.

  o There will be a scandal around Hillary Clinton and mail.

  o England's monarchy will end with Queen Elizabeth.[6]

- In June 2005, while a guest on *View Point* hosted by Mark Sims of Channel 19, Joseph predicted that Iran will not develop the bomb and peace will finally come about in the Middle East through pressure from the United States and Russia.[7]

- On a 2005 *River West Flowing* program hosted by Keith McDonald, Joseph predicted that riots lay ahead for the United States. He saw people struggling with unemployment, taxes, rising food costs and more, leading to revolts, *maybe even a revolution.*[8]

In addition, Joseph stated there will continue to be an increase in the monitoring of public activities and in the loss of personal freedoms as this country grows closer to becoming a police state.

MAHROO

For many years Joseph had been in contact with several spirit guides. While some preferred to remain nameless, one gave his name as "Godi." Another, an Indian medicine man, called himself "Broken Horn."

Joseph first had contact with Broken Horn while reading for a client in Tacoma, Washington. When he mentioned that he saw the spirit of an Indian with a broken horn on his head, the client jumped up from her chair, saying that while visiting Arizona, she had purchased a similar carving from an Indian tribe. She ran excitedly to the attic, retrieved it, and showed it to Joseph.

The figure was that of an American Indian. Carved out of wood, he was dressed in fur and had a pair of animal horns attached to the headpiece he wore. One of the horns that adorned the headpiece was broken.

At the end of the reading, the woman gave the carving to Joseph. When Joseph returned to Chicago, the spirit of Broken Horn began to come to him while he was in trance. As a medicine man, Broken Horn had also been a communicator of spirit.

When Joseph entered into trance and traveled out of his body, he communed with spirit. I asked him if he was ever afraid that something might happen to him while he was engaged in paranormal activities. He replied that he had no such fear, that his guides were always with him. He explained, "They protect me at all times, whether traveling out of body, meditating, in trance, performing an exorcism, or conducting a séance. My guides surround and protect me from malevolent entities."

One day Joseph told me that a master by the name of "Mahroo" (Joseph pronounced it Muh-roo), had appeared to him, introducing himself as an advanced and highly developed spirit guide. From the time of his creation, Mahroo has remained in spirit, having never incarnated into the physical world.

He appeared at a time when Joseph was to advance spiritually. Mahroo's charge was to work exclusively with Joseph for the express purpose of helping him reach the next level of his spiritual growth. Indeed, after the arrival of Mahroo, Joseph's work in healing, channeling, and guidance increased. From then on, Joseph worked solely with Mahroo. When Joseph performed a healing or communicated with a departed soul, Mahroo stepped in to assist him.

Whenever Joseph called on Mahroo, he appeared instantly, ready to help. Since time presents no barrier in the spiritual realm, being in two separate locations simultaneously—a phenomenon known as bilocation—posed no problem for Mahroo. Through the phenomenon of bilocation, he was able to appear in two places at once, making it possible to help souls on the astral plane while simultaneously guiding Joseph in his quest for spiritual knowledge. Mahroo had evolved to a state of finely vibrating energy—pure energy oscillating at a frequency so high it emits light.

Religions of the world equate light with spirituality; associating it with goodness. The Christian faith maintains that Christ was born to be the light of the world, fulfilling God's proclamation "Let there be light." Judaism rekindles the miracle of faith triumphing over evil in the celebration of Hanukkah, the Festival of Lights. During Kwanzaa, the secular celebration of black culture, seven candles, symbolic of the celebration's seven principles, rise from wooden stands meant to recall the people's roots in Africa. Hindus, Sikhs, and Jains light lanterns and small earthen lamps during Diwali to awaken awareness of God and the triumph of good over evil. Muslims refer to Allah as the source of light, providing inspiration, motivation, and guidance.[9]

Being a highly advanced spirit of light, Mahroo could slow the speed of his vibrations to become visible to Joseph. The first time he appeared, he took the form of a business person dressed in a smart suit and tie, yet he had the look of a scholar, a wise soul in possession of infinite knowledge.

Mahroo answered many of Joseph's clients' questions, often before they were asked. In addition to channeling information to Joseph's mind, Mahroo provided Joseph with clues. When conveying a message pertaining to a certain country, Mahroo would appear dressed in the garb of the region to enhance the answers he brought. At times he showed up in a turban, a feathered headdress, a toga, or a barrister's wig. Sometimes he came charging in on an Arabian stallion or riding a camel or an elephant. Mahroo obviously had a sense of the theatrical!

The different ways in which Mahroo appeared gave Joseph clues to the answer he was seeking for a particular client. Yet the interpretation was left to Joseph, not always an easy task.

Mahroo seemed to enjoy demonstrating his answers. He appeared in a variety of scenarios, often engaged in an activity or a sport. One time he arrived paddling a canoe upriver against the current. Joseph interpreted this to mean the path ahead would be difficult for his client. On another occasion he rode a bicycle downhill, coasting and pedaling with ease to show that the path would be easy. Walking on stilts or riding a unicycle indicated the need to take great care when attempting a certain action.

Mahroo brought many visions, some of them pertaining solely to Joseph. In one of these, Mahroo appeared dressed in battle fatigues with wisps of smoke coming off his clothing as he emerged from a fog-shrouded war scene complete with the sound of bombs exploding and machine guns spattering gunfire in the distance. He had come straight from battle, his face blackened with grease, to demonstrate his task of tending to souls who were killed violently. Mahroo was giving Joseph a clue to the work he would one day perform—helping souls cross to the other side.

Not every message Mahroo brought was serious or earth-shattering. Often he spoke of simple, everyday matters that pertained to Joseph or me or our families—events that were currently happening in our lives.

When I was present at a meditation session, I would end each session by asking Mahroo if he had anything more to tell us. One answer he gave, although simple, was noteworthy. Mahroo said that in the future music would not be the music we knew, that it was going to change. The ballads and melodies we enjoyed would take a backseat to something he didn't really consider to be music. Mahroo gave us this insight before the advent of synthesized computer-generated music and long before the dawn of rap, hip-hop, and other modern-day forms of composition.

While normally it would take much skill and a great deal of work for Mahroo to slow his vibrations and make a connection with those in the physical world, when Joseph relaxed his mind and entered an altered state, Mahroo found it easy to communicate with him. Joseph's command of meditation made Mahroo's channeling effortless.

From the beginning of their relationship, Mahroo and Joseph worked as a team—partners in bringing messages of comfort and spiritual blessings to countless numbers of people seeking answers, including me.

BLESSINGS AND HEALINGS

M ahroo led Joseph to a new level of spirituality. Joseph now focused more of his attention on spiritual matters and the further development of his ability as a direct trance medium, life coach, and spiritual counselor.

When someone came to Joseph for a healing, he first prayed with the individual, asking God to give his blessing, saying aloud: "Father, you who gave us the promise of healing, send your healing light through me, your faithful and abiding servant Joseph, to bring relief to this deserving soul. Father, we pray for this blessing in your holy name. Amen."

Next he channeled Mahroo and, speaking aloud, called on St. Joseph, asking for his presence and assistance throughout the ritual. Mahroo and St. Joseph then joined to bring in the healing light. Mahroo transmitted the light energy to Joseph, who in turn became the instrument that delivered the healing to the ailing person.

As the healing proceeded, Joseph would spread his fingers apart while passing his hands in a circular motion above the area of the disorder. As he worked, he slowly and gradually brought his fingers together as if forming a vacuum to capture and draw the ailment from the person's body. Closing his hands and turning away from the person, he'd next fling the disorder into the ether. Before ending the session, Joseph would recite the following final prayer:

> "Father, you who know the wrongs we have done and yet promised
> forgiveness, release this person from their suffering and restore their
> health. Father, we pray for this blessing in your holy name. Amen."

Joseph was adamant in telling his clients that the healing didn't come from him but from their faith in God. He would stress, "Healing is given through a person's faith. It is your belief that heals you."

Although Mahroo took on the role of conduit during a healing, his role changed when Joseph channeled a departed soul. In those instances, Mahroo became a gatekeeper and Joseph became the gateway. When departed souls discovered the gateway [Joseph], many rushed to get messages through to loved ones they left behind. At these times, Mahroo would organize and transmit the messages so Joseph could receive them in an orderly manner rather than jumbled together.

Joseph remarked on how happy the departed souls were to be in touch with those they had left behind. The souls were ecstatic when they were able to reach their loved ones, especially with a message that identified them and gave proof of their continued existence.

One day I asked Joseph if he would contact my mother for me. He sat back in a reclining chair, put his feet up, closed his eyes, and remained silent as he breathed deeply. After a few minutes, he informed me that my mother was there.

I told her how much I loved her and how I missed her. I then asked if she would give a sign by which I could know that I was in touch with her. With this, Joseph took several more deep breaths and said my mother was showing him something that looked like a tool of some kind. She was sitting under a tree on a warm summer's day with a large washtub on the ground in front of her. She showed him how happy she was and held up a bottle in one hand; in the other was a utensil of some kind that Joseph didn't recognize. He wasn't sure what she was doing and asked me if I knew.

I most certainly did!

One summer my mother decided to make homemade root beer. She was very excited about it, and when the time came to cap the bottles, we children begged her to let us help. However, she explained we were not old enough and saved that part for herself. Capping the bottles brought her great joy, and it was the utensil used to cap the bottles that Joseph saw but could not identify. As it turned out, the root beer was terrible. It was so bad we ended up dumping out every bottle— something we kids thoroughly enjoyed doing.

I realized my mother had sent me a perfect sign. No one other than me or another family member could have known about that adventure, and I most certainly had not thought about it since that summer many years before.

Weeks later, at my request, Joseph again contacted my mother. He saw her working in a flower garden. I wasn't quite sure this was a sign from her; many people love flowers. However, at the time of the reading, my brother was about to put my parents' house up for sale. My mother seemed concerned about this, so Joseph threw out a number for which he felt the house would sell.

Immediately upon saying this, he covered both of his ears and winced. He asked me if my mother used a cane. I told him no, to which he said, "Well, she found something to bang to get my attention as she shouted, 'That price is too low!'" He smiled, adding, "I don't know how she did it, but the noise was extremely loud. My ears are *still* ringing."

Shortly after that, my mother mentioned that her brother would soon be joining her. "In fact," she said, "he may already be here." When I asked if he was there now, she said she would have to check. (I later found out my uncle had passed away around the time that Joseph channeled my mother.)

Slowly and painfully, my mother rose from the flower bed she was tending and rubbed her knees. At first, Joseph was surprised. He didn't believe we carried over infirmities on passing. I wasn't surprised, however, since my mother suffered greatly from arthritis.

Joseph explained that he didn't feel she was really in pain; rather, she was giving me added proof she was alive. It was her way of doing something I would be sure to recognize.

Months later, in a third channeling session, my mother asked Joseph to tell me, "Over here we don't have to worry about our hair. We can fix it in any style we like." This had special meaning for me. My mother's hair was very thin and fine, so much so that it refused to cooperate. Styling it was easy; the problem was holding the style. We would roll her hair, back-comb it, tease and spray it, but no matter what we did the first bit of humidity rendered it flat. Even though I gave her home permanents, her hair remained difficult to manage.

My mother then complained about the people who bought her house. She said she wished they would clean up the backyard and keep it tidy. She had kept it immaculate.

I later asked my brother about this [he lived next door]. He confirmed that it was a mess. Once again, my mother's distinct personality had come through. She had managed to find unique ways to communicate to me that she still existed.

By channeling my dear mother, Joseph brought me hope, just as he brought hope to many others.

A GLIMPSE OF THE OTHER SIDE

Joseph told me that when a soul departs from the world, it passes through a number of dimensions before arriving at the level appropriate to its state of advancement. Once there, it resides with souls of like development and continues to grow and learn. The more advanced the soul, the higher the level reached and the finer and lighter its astral body.

Joseph's out-of-body travels allowed him to view the beauty of the spirit world. He spoke in awe of the unimaginable splendor, telling me that love permeates everything; the atmosphere just naturally absorbs it.

Joseph found great solace in the spirit planes. While in trance he was able to converse with me, and I would question him about the things he saw. However, whenever observing the afterlife, Joseph always directed me to intervene and "call him back" should he linger. The happiness and love he found there was so blissful that at times he had to force his return to the physical world. During a special series of trance sessions, Joseph visited and observed the realm of spirit, focusing on the afterlife.

Following are the comments he relayed to me:

- Picture yourself awakening in a peaceful and harmonious city filled with love and happiness. What a wonderful feeling of freedom you experience. You're free to float on the breeze should you wish. Gravity has no effect on you now, nor does time. Spend as long as you wish; there's no need to rush.

- People mingle outside their homes and inside community centers. These centers, where one can meditate and pray, dot the serene landscape. Wherever you look, families and friends join and befriend others who are new to the community. They gather for fun, work, companionship, learning, and sharing.

- Enormous learning centers—great halls filled with books containing universal knowledge—occupy the center of the city. Here higher souls can be found enlightening and helping others, providing aid, guidance, and understanding when a soul requests to experience a lesson it needs for spiritual growth.

- Substance in the spirit world is quite supple; objects are easily materialized. Here you find work is accomplished mentally. Everything is built through the power of thought. As Joseph would say: "Mind is the contractor; thought the builder."

- Imagine what it would be like to create things by simply using your mind. At first you may be tempted to the create things you've always desired, but like a kid in a candy store, you find that overwhelming. You discover that giving brings more blessings than receiving, and soon realize the greatest happiness is found in the joy of giving to others.

- The construction of houses is accomplished through the many souls who stop by to pitch in and help. You'll find them willing to lend a hand—or rather, a "thought."

- Homes are not like those we find on earth. Their walls are translucent and absorb the warm glow of beautifully colored hues that stream down from the sky.

- Surrounding each home and building are beds of flowers—flowers of indescribable designs and unbelievable colors—shapes and colors we've not yet seen or imagined. Their fragrance fills the air. As you pass by, you notice each flower seems to delight in your enjoyment. The petals of the flowers are exceptionally beautiful. They appear to be transparent, able to absorb the surrounding rays of color. Suddenly a gentle breeze blows, changing the bent of the petals. Now opaque, the petals reflect rays of colors back up to the sky.

- Soft music fills the air, mingling with the melody of magnificently colored songbirds flying above. When they come to rest, they sit in trees heavily laden with ripened fruits at the peak of perfection—just waiting for your enjoyment. Pick your choice; each tree bears an amazing assortment of fruit.

- Streams of sparkling water flow gently among hills and valleys filled with trees and foliage. The grass is a vivid green with varying textures, more perfect than that of any golf course.

Joseph explained that newly arrived souls might find this a bit overwhelming, but they soon discover they are able to control their individual environment—to subdue or change these marvels to fit their desire.

"Control of personal space is accomplished through one's own will," he reiterated. "Most souls immerse themselves in their new surroundings quickly. Others take more time, gradually awakening to the unfamiliar yet perfect environment. A soul eventually feels oneness with everything, finding perfect love and harmony within that oneness."

Joseph said the Golden Rule—"Do unto others as you would have others do unto you"— applies also in the spirit world and actually is more applicable there. By honoring this rule, a soul in the spirit world may advance spiritually.

A soul following its desire to advance will eventually seek its own path. It may choose to gain enlightenment from the teachings of a master or through studying the books of knowledge in the great halls of learning. Alternatively, it may choose to review its recent life and discover how its choices influenced others, even perceiving the effects different choices would have had.

In his out-of-body travels, Joseph discovered that all souls seek fulfillment; they search for the universal consciousness found in God's love. Eventually they come to understand that, as his children, we are trying to become perfect in God's eyes. All souls, he insisted, seek the ultimate fulfillment—to join God. Of course, when we think of the afterlife, we think of love and peace, which perfectly describes Joseph's findings in the higher dimensions.

Ultimately, Joseph advised people to live in this life as they wished to live in the next—in a way that advances and increases spiritual awareness. He observed, "The higher the dimension, the greater is the peace, beauty, and love." He urged those curious about the afterlife to remember: "At all times, you are spirit. Whether on the other side in an astral body or here on earth in a physical body—it matters not—*the real you is spirit.*"

Spiritual Underpinnings

During many of my Saturday talks with Joseph, the conversation would turn to Joseph's childhood and his grandfather's teachings about the spiritual underpinnings of life. I began to notice that when he spoke of these, Joseph often made mention of God's blessings and God's loving relationship with us, his children. To hear God spoken of in this way was a revelation to me. The people who populated my town were holier-than-thou Roman Catholics, Methodists, and Episcopalians—"High Episcopalians," as they were quick to point out. The Sunday sermons in these churches spilled over with fear, fire, and brimstone. Talk of God was invariably about his judgment and wrath, along with constant reminders of the punishments he doled out. Considering him angry and unapproachable, I'd spent much of my childhood keeping God at a distance.

How different it was to hear Joseph speaking of a God who loved us and put each of us on earth to learn and grow. I was excited to hear more about this loving God.

Joseph taught me that God wants us to be joyful and successful since success is part of happiness. He taught me that God wants us to know him and have a personal relationship with him because he takes special interest in each of us. Joseph often reminded me that we each have a purpose in being here and that God wants us to reach out and fulfill that purpose.

I really enjoyed it when Joseph had time to talk and share these things with me. However, one Saturday morning during the summer of 2006 brought more than I anticipated.

A Warning from Mahroo

Most people with ESP tend to specialize in a certain area. Mediums communicate with the dead; psychics read energy fields surrounding a person; clairvoyants are able to see visions; clairaudients hear messages from beyond; shamans have the gift of healing. Joseph was endowed with the ability to perform all of these functions. In addition, he developed the power of his mind when astral traveling, enhancing his ability to explore the world of spirit while out-of-body.

Curiously, being able to witness tragic events seemed a strange fate for a man such as Joseph, whose teachings centered on love and peace. Even so, he refused to take on the role of alarmist. No matter what he saw or how ominous it appeared, he spoke of it thoughtfully, cushioning his words and removing any sense of fear.

There are always some who predict the end of the world is coming, but Joseph was not one of them. In fact, when questioned about the end of the world, he took advantage of the opportunity to tell people, "the world itself will not end; however, the world *as we know it* will." He'd repeat the sentence and add the word *period* at the end to emphasize his certainty. In this case he would say, "The world itself will not end; however, the world *as we know it* will—*Period.*" Joseph often added the word *period* at the end of a sentence when wanting to make a point.

Never a fearmonger, Joseph startled me one Saturday morning when he looked me in the eye and somberly said, "I don't want to alarm you, but I have something to tell you." Never before had Joseph begun a conversation with me so seriously. I knew from the sound of his voice that what he was going to say would be unsettling.

Normally when Joseph saw something upsetting, he would cushion it by saying, "I've got something to tell you. It's not so good, but you shouldn't worry about it," or "I had a disturbing vision last night, but you know there's always a chance I can be wrong." This time, no qualifying statement followed.

Joseph continued in the same solemn manner as he told me, "Things on earth are going to get bad—really bad." He hesitated a moment and then repeated his words. This time Joseph put a great deal of emphasis on the words *really bad*. He went on to say, "This is just the beginning; misery and sorrow will be with us for many years." He added, "Things will seem to be getting better, but then they'll get worse and it won't only be here. This time the entire world is going to be involved; no one will be spared. Tragedy will touch people everywhere in one way or another. There's no escaping what's ahead."

As he spoke, I could tell Joseph was psychically feeling the pain and the suffering others would experience. I struggled to understand what he was telling me; this sounded nothing like his earlier messages. It was out of character for him to be so somber and speak with such finality. This wasn't the gentle, fun-loving, don't-take-life-too-seriously Joseph I had known.

"What do you mean *bad*—how bad?" I asked. "What did you see? Why are you talking like this?"

Reluctantly, Joseph revealed a message that Mahroo had brought him a few weeks earlier—a message which he hadn't yet shared with me. The message was about the future and what lies ahead for the world.

Joseph told me Mahroo had shown him a picture of the world sitting on a powder keg that was about to explode. Mahroo had told him, "The time is close. The world is sitting on a ticking time-bomb and time is running out. Changes are about to come that will bring turmoil and despair." Even more unsettling, Mahroo told Joseph, "The world need no longer wait for Tribulation; a time of great suffering and sorrow has already begun. A time of woe is upon us now, and it brings with it death, suffering, hardship, and remorse." He added, "Remember, the suffering is man-made. It's caused by man's greed, lust for power, and irreverence for life."

Mahroo's warning didn't seem to affect Joseph other than the thought of people suffering and that he hated to be the bearer of bad news. However, it had a profound effect on me. I fought against even the idea of accepting it.

While aware that many people in the world were already suffering greatly, not once had I stopped to think that a dire future could be upon us right now. To me, this seemed like something that belonged far off in the future. *That's where it belongs*, I thought. *Great suffering and sorrow are out there in the future, not here and now.*

I wanted to continue talking to Joseph about Mahroo's message, but it would be many days before the chance arose.

GOOD-BYE

T he following Saturday when I arrived at the office, Joseph immediately announced that he wanted to go into trance. Pen in hand, I waited while he relaxed thinking he would continue telling me more about Mahroo's message. Each time Joseph channeled Mahroo, out of curiosity I would ask what Mahroo was doing. This time Joseph replied, "He's just sitting there on a log, waiting for me to catch up."

I thought this was a strange thing for Joseph to say and jotted a note to ask him about it later when suddenly Joseph emerged from his trance. I asked him what Mahroo meant by "he's waiting for you to catch up," but Joseph managed to deflect my question by showing me a new publicity piece he was planning to use. We spent the rest of the morning working on it.

The next few weeks passed quickly. Time flew by and then suddenly, without warning, Joseph became ill. Ever since his heart surgery, Joseph had been healthy and robust, but now he was having difficulty breathing.

Joseph was hospitalized and treated with antibiotics, after which a cardiac surgeon performed angioplasty to widen one of his heart valves. After a week's stay, he was sent home with orders to take another round of antibiotics, but within three days of release Joseph was back in the emergency room suffering severe chills and even greater difficulty breathing.

He called me from the emergency room and said he would be admitted as soon as a room became available; he was having "the kind of chills where you can't get warm no matter what you do." Joseph told me they had started him on an IV, a different antibiotic, and oxygen. I told him not to worry—the hospital staff would take good care of him and I would be there as soon as I could. With that he said he had to hang up then since the doctor had come in to see him.

Sadly, this was the last conversation that Joseph and I would have.

Shortly after he was admitted, Joseph's breathing became even more labored, making it necessary to put him on a ventilator. With a tube in his throat, he was unable to speak. From then on, our conversations were one-sided. I did the talking and in response he would nod his head or squeeze my hand. Most of the time the doctors kept him sedated, making communication impossible.

Very soon the antibiotics ceased to be effective, and Joseph developed pneumonia. Apparently he had contracted a streptococcal infection during his initial stay in the hospital, and now it was full-blown and resistant to medication.

Over the next few weeks several attempts were made to wean Joseph from the ventilator, but to no avail. His body was simply too weak to breathe without assistance. Eventually the infection spread to his blood, and septicemia set in. Despite the dialysis treatments he received, the sepsis attacked one organ after another—liver, lungs, kidneys, and heart. But with every setback Joseph rallied, giving us hope that eventually he would recover.

Throughout this stressful time, many people kept a close vigil over Joseph. No one was more attentive than his beloved son, Joseph Jr., and Richard Kemp, a dear friend of Joseph's. They took turns remaining at Joseph's bedside night and day. His daughter Linda, caretaker Pat, and I, along with many other friends and family members also visited. Never was Joseph left alone; someone was always by his side.

Amy, who had moved, was on the phone each day, faithfully checking on her beloved "father." Unable to be with him in person, she, along with the rest of us, suffered greatly.

Many people were praying for him, but sadly he did not recover. Joseph passed from this world in the same way which he entered it—slowly and with much difficulty.

In retrospect, I'm certain that when Mahroo told Joseph he was waiting for him to catch up, Joseph knew he was going to die. I'm also certain that the reason Joseph dodged my question about the meaning of Mahroo's "waiting for him to catch up" message was that he did not want to burden others with the knowledge that he would soon be joining Mahroo in the spirit world.

CONCLUSION:

MESSAGES FROM
BEYOND THE GRAVE

J oseph's passing greatly saddened his family as well as his friends, countless
clients, and, of course, me. Although in my heart I knew that he lived on, I
was overwhelmed with grief. After many long and painful months, my need to
hear from Joseph felt suddenly urgent so I called upon world-famous medium
Hans Christian King, renowned for speaking with the dead. It felt strange to
contemplate seeking advice from another medium, so I was careful not to reveal
any personal details, giving King's secretary only my first name.

I was soon at Hans King's office in North Carolina for the first of two
in-person readings. With no foreknowledge of Joseph or information about me,
Hans brought me a message that convinced me he was in touch with Joseph. He
began by telling me that spirit was saying I should do automatic writing. But no
sooner had the words come out of his mouth than Hans stopped and said, "No,
wait. That's not it." He then closed his eyes, cocked his head to one side, and
appeared to be listening to a voice. On opening his eyes, Hans said the message
he received was not that I should do automatic writing but that I should "write—
write the book." I couldn't erase the smile from my face.

Hans asked if I had been planning to write a book. I then told him about
Joseph and his work, explaining that for many years I assisted him in his office.
I acknowledged that although I was doubtful whenever he said it, [Joseph always
told me I could be a writer], recently the thought of writing a book in Joseph's
memory had crossed my mind.

"Well, that explains it," Hans said. "Joseph is coming through and he is
insisting that I tell you that he wants you to write. And, he wants you to "do
it—do it soon."

Hans went on. "Joseph says to tell you he hasn't left you and that he'll help you. He wants you to know that wherever you are, he is—*period.*" Hans smiled and said, "He's emphasizing the word *period*. He says you will know what that means. Does that make sense to you?" he asked.

Did it ever! Adding the word *period* at the end of a sentence was Joseph's way of letting me know with certainty that this was him; that he was still alive. There was no doubt in my mind that Hans had contacted Joseph.

Hans brought me much comfort that day. He gave me a greater understanding of the departed. He pointed out that departed souls are eager to give us reassurance that they live, as eager as we are to know they're alive. Hans said, "They desire to let us know they're still with us, watching over us, sharing in the joy and the sadness of our lives." Hans explained that it is good to ask help from the departed, to give them something to work on. He added, "They're happy to be involved and eager to help us."

Hans's message about asking for help proved to be true. Ever since, whenever I've asked Joseph for help, he has brought me solutions to my struggles. For example, a few years after Joseph died, my husband and I were buying a house and I was torn between two that were for sale. Both had some features that I liked and others that I didn't. I was having a hard time deciding which one to make an offer on. I felt pressured, since we wanted to close on a house before the end of the year and time was running short.

One night before going to sleep, I decided to ask Joseph for his help. I cleared my mind, relaxed, and closed my eyes. Before long, Joseph delivered an image of me driving my car. I wondered about it and then promptly fell asleep. The next morning I thought about the image but still could not figure out what it meant. I decided that Joseph wanted me to drive so I got in my car and drove past each of the two houses, hoping to resolve my dilemma.

When I passed the first house, nothing seemed unusual and I concluded that perhaps Joseph didn't mean for me to drive past the houses but rather to understand that I was letting the decision drive me. Still, as the other house was nearby, I drove on. As I approached the second house, a flock of white birds flew out of a tree in the front yard and landed on the roof of the house. I pulled the car to the side of the street and watched as the birds took off and circled over my car before flying away. I knew then that this was the sign I was looking for. We ended up buying that house, which turned out to be a good decision.

As Hans continued with my reading, he told me about the work Joseph was doing. He said Joseph was helping those who had suffered traumatic deaths to cross over to the other side, where he received and comforted them. Hans compared it to the ancient Greek myth of departing souls being ferried across the River Styx by the boatman named Charon. In the myth, the River Styx separates the world of the living from the world of the dead and souls crossing the river arrive on the other side, near the gate to the afterlife.

"Now," said Hans, "as those who experience a traumatic death cross over, Joseph is there to receive and tend to them, healing and taking away any fear they may have." It comforted me to hear this special work had been assigned to Joseph. Hans said it was reserved for souls of advanced spiritual development.

Quite some time passed before I could bring myself to relax and still my mind, but eventually I was ready to write and sure enough Joseph was there beside me—as he said he would be—sending me reminders of details I'd forgotten; telepathically impressing his thoughts upon my mind. The words poured out as my fingers flew over the keyboard.

Many months later I went to see Hans a second time. Only this time, before going, I petitioned Joseph to let Hans know I was coming. I wanted to see if Joseph could again get through to Hans from the spirit world. I was anxious to find out if Hans would mention anything about it when I got there.

Upon making the appointment with Hans's secretary, I again gave only my first name. As I walked into his office, I noticed that Hans looked at me strangely. When I sat down he said, "It's you. For the past week, spirit has repeatedly sent me the message, 'She's coming—she's coming!' and I wondered who it was that was coming to see me."

Hans's words astounded me. Goose bumps rose on my arms, and shivers rippled up and down my spine. I knew immediately that Joseph had done what I had asked. He'd sent Hans the message just as I'd requested, communicating the undeniable proof of an afterlife, convincing me that, as he always said, "Our souls survive death. We go on living."

In this sitting, Hans told me that many souls had gathered and wanted to speak with me, including that of my mother, who was sending me her love. When he asked, "Who died from cancer?" I told him that my mother had.

Later in the reading, Hans asked once again, "Who is the lady who died of cancer? She's wearing a baseball cap and keeps pushing to the front, insisting that she wants to speak with you. She really wants to tell you something."

I then realized that it wasn't my mother—it was Donna, a colleague from my full-time job who was dearly loved by her coworkers. When she had become ill and died from ovarian cancer, all of us were deeply saddened. An avid Chicago

Cubs fan, she had requested that her family bury her in her "Cubbies" uniform. When we arrived at her wake, there she was, decked out in her beloved Chicago Cubs' uniform and cap. As she had asked, the many Cubs' memorabilia and souvenirs she'd collected over the years were in the coffin with her.

I informed Hans that it was Donna and relayed to him the story of her burial in full Cubs attire. He laughed and said, "Well, she really wants to tell you something. She's saying, "Work is a lot easier here. You just have to think about doing it and it's done. You use your mind to do work.'"

Later during the reading, I asked Hans about the apparition I had seen as a child. When I finished telling him of my experience, Hans was smiling. He looked me straight in the eyes and said, "In all the years I've been working with people, *never* has anyone told me what you just did." He went on to say that he had the same experience as a child, only he went with his guide when asked if he wanted to go. Hans explained that it was a master who had visited me, a master spirit guide. On hearing of Hans's experience, I was sorry I had not gone with my master spirit guide when invited. Now that I knew what it involved, the thought of astral travel appealed to me.

Giving it more thought, however, I realized how important it was that my master guide had found me! Surely the purpose of his visit was to bring a lonely child assurance that another world existed—the living, loving world of spirit.

I still feel Joseph with me, mostly through heightened sensory experiences. Often a familiar scent fills the air, like the aroma of the freshly brewed coffee that drifted into Joseph's hospital room whenever I would visit him there. While sitting at my desk to work on the book, the smell would envelop me like a cloak, remaining for hours.

One evening while sitting at my desk, I saw an orb of light about the size of large cantaloupe hovering just below the ceiling. It danced back and forth for about a minute and then disappeared. I had read about orbs but had never seen one. I knew right away that it was Joseph.

At times I hear his voice as well. When I began writing about the warning that Mahroo had sent us, Joseph brought his own message, showing me a vision of the Four Horsemen of the Apocalypse charging across the land. In my mind I could hear him say, "The Four Horsemen have been set free to ride across the earth. Their reins loosened, they're free to take their toll." He continued, impressing upon me, "The time of suffering has not yet ended. But remember, no matter what happens, this world is not going to end."

During such moments, I reflect on one or another of Joseph's visions of the future we had talked about in the months before he passed from earth:

- Hundreds of thousands of businesses and homes falling into foreclosure

- Detroit becoming the capital of a small nation resembling a police state

- Marriage becoming a business arrangement, guaranteeing the financial support of any children

- Rockets propelling large unmanned spaceships carrying supplies to space stations, with astronauts being transported separately in much smaller and safer spaceships

- Residential and commercial heat being generated by chemicals

- The development of a nonpolluting engine that burns a type of fuel capable of emitting water as a byproduct

- Colored light therapy being used to heal illness and disease

- Masks adorned with feathers, sequins, and semiprecious stones becoming commonplace—being worn to ward off disease

- Holograms projected into the sky and onto the land for military and other purposes

- Terrorists planning to deface Mount Rushmore

- Los Angeles and Houston becoming primary targets for terrorist activities

- An attack overseas involving the deployment of a limited number of nuclear bombs

- Growing unrest and turmoil as people struggle with unemployment, taxes, rising food costs and more, leading to riots, *maybe even a revolution.*

Whenever he spoke of these projections, Joseph would tell me not to worry, saying, "Many times the world has gone through devastating periods and we have always survived—humankind is resilient, even under the most difficult of circumstances." Or, "Many changes are coming and, along with them, growth. We'll see an end to war, an end to hunger, and a halt to suffering, poverty, and inequity."

So, when feeling his presence from beyond the grave and thinking about his visions of the future, I do not worry. I can hear him say, as he often had, "God is loving and patient. In the past, He has and He always will give us the chance to change. Remember, God is a forgiving God. He will give us the chance to make things right."

Unfortunately change usually comes out of personal necessity, not out of compassion for fellow human beings. Our creative juices don't seem to flow until we have a need or until a need becomes so great that the world can no longer ignore it by turning away its eyes. It was not until the price of gasoline started to creep higher that we seriously began to look for fuel sources other than oil and demanded alternative ways to produce more energy-efficient automobiles.

One day Joseph added adamantly, as he had in the past, "It's up to us. We have the power and the means to wipe out famine and disease, and it's certainly in the hands of man to put an end to war." A few minutes later he insisted I make it clear in the book that our world is not doomed to extinction. He cautioned that we not blame God for the coming sorrows, stating that, "It is man—not God—who brings these woes. These woes will come about because of man's greed for money, power and control."

"Remember, God never turns his back on us; it's we who turn away from him. God gave us a marvelous mind and a wonderful gift to use as we choose—*the gift of free will.* We can change things over which we have control, such as respect for life and help for those who are less fortunate."

Joseph spoke of wanting to prepare people to face the future. However, being prepared, he insisted, did not mean people should build bomb shelters, stock up on food and water, buy guns, put up fences, and isolate themselves from others.

"Instead," Joseph said, "we need to work together with one another to solve our problems. We need to become more family, community, and world oriented. One day, social standing will lose its importance. Regard for the preservation of humanity will become more important than social status.

"Nothing can be accomplished unless people the world over unite and cooperate to take the required action. Only through a concentrated worldwide effort will we be able to stave off otherwise certain calamity. People everywhere need to become caretakers of life, guardians of the world. Life on this planet is depending upon us."

Joseph foresaw the day when entire communities would turn toward a type of communal living in which people care for and support one another. He saw many services bartered for goods.

"Now is the time to act, he advised—to do everything in our power to perfect our souls. No one knows who among us may fall victim to tragedy. Strengthening our character bodes us well under any circumstance."

Joseph ended his message by saying, "Tell people to follow the path that leads to peace."

NOTES

Part I

1. According to numerous firsthand reports, a huge feathered creature with red eyes, resembling a man with the face of a moth, had terrorized the town of Point Pleasant, West Virginia, prior to the bridge collapse. Those who encountered it were shaken to the core as the creature with a wingspan of eight to ten feet dive-bombed them at tremendous speed. A creature similar in appearance has been seen in different parts of the world, always prior to a tragedy. The presence of Mothman, still dreaded, is considered a predecessor to disaster.

2. "What Psychics See for 1969," *Midwest Magazine,* Sunday supplement of the *Chicago Sun-Times,* November 29, 1968.

3. Harold Hill interview in *National Insider,* August 15, 1971.

4. Joseph Stimac interview, "Chicago Psychic Predicts 2 Major Disasters—And They Come True" *National Enquirer,* May 25, 1969

5. David Techter, "Chicago Psychic Predicts 2 Major Disasters—And They Come True," *National Enquirer,* May 25, 1969

6. Arnold Weissmann, "Tales of the Psychic City," *Reader* 5, no. 30 (April 30, 1976).

7. Jennifer L. Goss, "Ted Kennedy and the Chappaquiddick Accident," http://history1900s.about.com/od/1960s/s/Chappaquiddick.html.

8. A truncated version of the televised exorcism can be viewed online at www.youtube.com/watch?v=y-6j3s65kC8.

9. Chicago radio WGN, July 12, 1987.

10. *PM Magazine,* June 1986 live television broadcast of Joseph walking the floor of the Chicago Board of Trade.

11. Mary Neiswender, "Psychics Give Tate Case Ideas," *Independent Press-Telegram*, August 21, 1969. Copyright 1969 by *Independent Press-Telegram*.

12. Ibid.

13. Neiswender, "Psychic Described Tate 'Thrill Killers,'" *Independent Press-Telegram*, December 3, 1969. Copyright 1969 by *Independent Press-Telegram*.

14. Ibid.

15. Neiswender, "Psychic Predicts Missing Manson Attorney Is Dead," *Independent Press-Telegram*, December 9, 1970. Copyright 1970 by *Independent Press-Telegram*.

16. Ibid.

17. Bud Kressin, "Zodiac May Give Up Today, Seer Says," *Vallejo Times-Herald*, January 4, 1970. Copyright 1970 by *Vallejo Times-Herald*.

Part II

1. Prov. 23:7 (World English Bible).

2. David Kaiser, *How the Hippies Saved Physics: Science, Counterculture, and the Quantum Revival* (New York: W. W. Norton, 2011): Ch. 2.

3. Hugh C. Boyle, Bishop of Pittsburgh, *Roman Catholic Church Pamphlet.*

Part III

1. Cynthia Austin interview, "River West Flowing," Chicago TV Channel 19, October 15, 2002.

2. Ibid.

3. Ibid.

4. Ibid.

5. Ibid.

6. Ibid.

Part IV

1. Cliff Kelly interview, Chicago radio WVON, June 1989.

2. Art Bell interview, *Coast to Coast*, Chicago's WLS, January 11, 1999.

3. Marc Sims interview, "View Point," Chicago TV Channel 19, June 2001.

4. Cynthia Austin and Leonard Grady interview, "River West Flowing," Chicago TV Channel 19, November 2001.

5. Sports anchor, Chicago 9 Evening News, 2003.

6. Joseph DeLouise (self-interview), "River West Flowing," Chicago TV Channel 19, 2005.

7. Marc Sims interview, "View Point," Chicago, Channel 19, June 2005.

8. Keith McDonald interview, "River West Flowing," Chicago TV Channel 19, 2005.

9. "A Beacon of Hope: The Importance of Light in Religion," last modified 12/23/2011, usatoday30.usatoday.com/news/...of...light-in-religion/.../1/.

Bibliography

Anderson, Jack, and Darly Gibson. *Peace, War, and Politics: An Eyewitness Account.* New York: Forge, 1999.

Bly, Nellie. *The Kennedy Men: Three Generations of Sex, Scandal, and Secrets.* New York: Kensington Books, 1996.

Damore, Leo. *Senatorial Privilege: The Chappaquiddick Cover-up.* New York: Dell Publishing, 1989.

Defano, M. M. *The Living Prophets.* New York: Dell Publishing, 1972.

DeLouise, Joseph. "It's All in Your Mind." *Coronet Magazine,* May 1973.

Encyclopedia of Occultism & Parapsychology, Predictor: Joseph DeLouise, 5th ed., s.v., 1975.

Godwin, John. *Occult America.* New York: Doubleday, 1971.

Graysmith, Robert, *Zodiac,* St. Martin's Press, 1986, The Berkley Group, 1987. and *Zodiac Unmasked: The Identity of America's Most Illusive Serial Killer Revealed,* The Berkley Publishing Group, The Penguin Group, 2002, 2007.

Greenhouse, Herbert B. *Premonitions: A Leap Into the Future.* New York: Bernard Geis Associates, 1971.

Holzer, Hans. *Directory of Psychics: How to Find, Evaluate, and Communicate with Professional Psychics and Mediums.* Chicago: Contemporary Books, 1995.

Kaiser, David. *How the Hippies Saved Physics: Science, Counterculture, and the Quantum Revival.* New York: W. W. Norton & Company, 2011.

Melton, J. Gordon, ed. *Encyclopedia of Occultism & Parapsychology*, 5th ed., vol. 1, A-L, 2001.

Neiswender, Mary. *Long Beach Press-Telegram*, 1969.

Olsen, Jack. *The Bridge at Chappaquiddick.* Boston: Little, Brown, 1970.

Steiger, Brad. Psychic City Chicago. New York: Doubleday, 1976.

Wallechinsky, David, and Amy Wallace. The Book of Lists: The Original Compendium of Curious *Information*. Toronto, Canada: Random House of Canada, 1977.

ILLUSTRATION CREDITS

Figure 1. From "ESP 'vision' of bridge disaster told," by David Techter, *New Age World*, March 1968, p. 12. Copyright 1968 by *New Age World*.

Figure 2. From Broadcast transcript, St. Louis radio station SKSLQ, November 14, 1978.

Figure 3. From "Psychic 'Reads' Tomorrow's Newspaper – Today," by Lois Czubakowski, *The Prospect Day*, September 12, 1969. Copyright 1969 by *The Prospect Day*.

About the Author

M ary Lou Emami has personal experience with extrasensory perception. When she was eight, she came upon the apparition of a ghostly man bearing a distinct question for her. This event was followed by other phenomena— a near-death experience at the bottom of a swimming pool, an eerie out-of-body event, a frightening automatic writing incident, vivid dreams, and forewarnings of future happenings, including one that told of personal danger. Her premonitions continued after marriage.

Becoming aware of Joseph DeLouise's psychic powers, she volunteered to assist him in his office, where, for over twenty years, she observed this principled man helping others. She took notes, composed and sent news releases, and created publicity and marketing pieces. Over the years, she and Joseph often talked of his amazingly accurate predictions and the stories behind each of them.

Mary Lou worked as a training consultant, marketing workplace training programs to business and manufacturing companies. She served on the board of directors for the Glendale Heights, Illinois Chamber of Commerce for eight years. Seven years ago, Mary Lou and a colleague opened their own training consulting business.

Mary Lou and her husband enjoy traveling, the company of good friends, weekend excursions, and visits with their children in Illinois and Florida, where their eight "go-to" internet-and-social-media-savvy grandchildren lovingly keep them up-to-date.

If you enjoyed reading this book and you feel Joseph's words might help others, kindly consider writing a review for *Psychic Courier* on Amazon.

Thank you.

http://psychiccourier.com

http://marylouemami.com